Teacher's Guide

PATHWAYS

Listening, Speaking, and Critical Thinking

1

Becky Tarver Chase

NATIONAL GEOGRAPHIC LEARNING | HEINLE CENGAGE Learning

Australia • Brazil • Japan • Korea • Mexico • Singapore • Spain • United Kingdom • United States

Pathways 1 Teacher's Guide
Listening, Speaking, and Critical Thinking
Becky Tarver Chase

Publisher: Sherrise Roehr

Executive Editor: Laura Le Dréan

Acquisitions Editor: Tom Jefferies

Development Editor: Marissa Petrarca

Director of Global Marketing: Ian Martin

Marketing Manager: Caitlin Thomas

Marketing Manager: Emily Stewart

Director of Content and Media Production:
Michael Burggren

Senior Content Project Manager: Daisy Sosa

Manufacturing Manager: Marcia Locke

Manufacturing Buyer: Marybeth Hennebury

Cover Design: Page 2 LLC

Cover Image: Raul Touzon/National
Geographic Image Collection

Interior Design: Page 2 LLC, Cenveo Publisher
Services/Nesbitt Graphics, Inc.

Composition: Cenveo Publisher Services/
Nesbitt Graphics, Inc.

ISBN-13: 978-1-111-83228-5

ISBN-10: 1-111-83228-5

National Geographic Learning
20 Channel Center St.
Boston, MA 02210
USA

Cengage Learning is a leading provider of customized learning solutions with office locations around the globe, including Singapore, the United Kingdom, Australia, Mexico, Brazil, and Japan. Locate your local office at:
international.cengage.com/region

Cengage Learning products are represented in Canada by Nelson Education, Ltd.

Visit National Geographic Learning online at **www.ngl.cengage.com**
Visit our corporate website at **www.cengage.com**

Printed in the United States of America
2 3 4 5 6 7 8 15 14 13 12

TABLE OF CONTENTS

Advantages of *Pathways Listening, Speaking, and Critical Thinking*

In *Pathways Listening, Speaking, and Critical Thinking*, real-world content from *National Geographic* publications provides a context for meaningful language acquisition. Students learn essential, high-frequency vocabulary, review important grammatical structures, and practice listening and speaking skills that will allow them to succeed in both academic and social settings.

Pathways Listening, Speaking, and Critical Thinking can be used in a wide variety of language-learning programs, from high schools and community colleges to private institutes and intensive English programs. The high-interest content motivates students and teachers alike.

The following features are included in *Pathways Listening, Speaking, and Critical Thinking*:

- Academic Pathways give students and teachers clear performance objectives for each unit.

- Opening pages introduce the unit theme and provide key vocabulary and concepts.

- Interesting content is used to present target vocabulary and to spark discussions.

- Extensive audio programs include lectures, interviews, conversations, and pronunciation models that expose students to many different kinds of speakers.

- Clear grammar charts present key grammar structures and explain language functions such as asking for clarification and sustaining a conversation.

- Presentation Skills boxes highlight skills for planning and delivering successful oral presentations.

- Student to Student boxes provide real-world expressions for making friends and working with classmates.

- An *Independent Student Handbook* and vocabulary index at the end of each level serve as tools to use in class or for self-study and review.

Teaching Language Skills and Academic Literacy

Students need more than language skills to succeed in an academic setting. In addition to teaching the English language, the *Pathways* series teaches academic literacy, which includes not only reading, writing, speaking, and listening skills, but also visual literacy, classroom participation and collaboration skills, critical thinking, and the ability to use technology for learning. Students today are expected to be motivated, inquisitive, original, and creative. In short, they're expected to possess quite an extensive skill set before they even begin their major course of study.

Using *National Geographic* Content in a Language Class

The use of high-interest content from *National Geographic* publications sets the *Pathways* series apart. Instead of working with topics that might seem irrelevant, students are engaged by fascinating stories about real people and places around the world and the issues that affect us all.

High-interest content is introduced throughout each unit—as context for target vocabulary, as content for lectures and conversation—and provides the information students need for lively discussions and interesting presentations.

The topics in the *Pathways Listening, Speaking, and Critical Thinking* series correspond to academic subject areas and appeal to a wide range of interests. For example:

Academic Subject Area	Unit Title	Unit Theme
Health Science	*Inside the Brain*	the physiology and psychology of the human brain
History/Archaeology	*Treasures from the Past*	recent underwater discoveries and the lessons they impart about the value of history
Anthropology/Sociology	*Culture and Tradition*	traditions from cultures around the world, from cowboys to Caribbean music
Earth Science	*Fascinating Planet*	the geography and geology of national parks in China, Brazil, Madagascar, and New Zealand
Economics/Business	*Making a Living, Making a Difference*	economic development including cooperatives, cottage industries, entrepreneurs, and charitable organizations

Increasing Visual Literacy

Photographs, maps, charts, and graphs can all convey enormous amounts of information. Lecturers and professors rarely give oral presentations without some kind of visual aid. Helping students to make sense of visuals is an important part of preparing them for academic success.

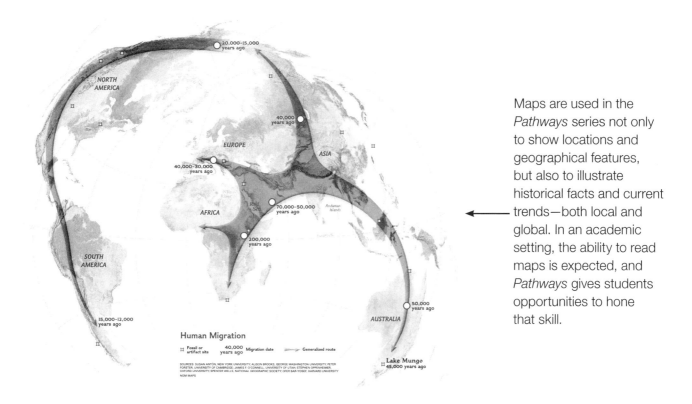

Maps are used in the *Pathways* series not only to show locations and geographical features, but also to illustrate historical facts and current trends—both local and global. In an academic setting, the ability to read maps is expected, and *Pathways* gives students opportunities to hone that skill.

Charts and graphs present numerical data in a visual way, and the *Pathways* series gives students practice in reading them. In addition to the standard pie charts and bar graphs, *Pathways* includes more unusual visuals from the pages of *National Geographic* publications.

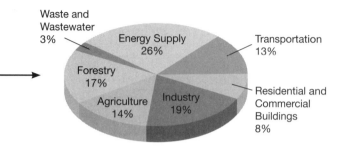

Graphic organizers have several functions in the *Pathways* series. They appeal to visual learners by showing relationships between ideas in a visual way. So, in addition to texts and listening passages, *Pathways* uses graphic organizers to present interesting content. Students are asked to use graphic organizers for a number of academic tasks such as generating topics or organizing notes for a presentation.

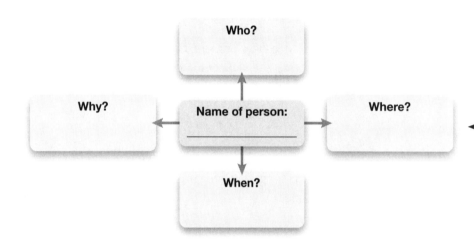

The photographs in the *Pathways* series go far beyond decorating the pages. Photographs introduce the unit theme and provide necessary background information for understanding listening passages and texts. Teachers will also want to exploit the photographs in *Pathways* to initiate discussions and reinforce the target language.

Building Critical Thinking Skills

Critical thinking skills are explicitly taught and practiced in *Pathways Listening, Speaking, and Critical Thinking*. One reason for this is that critical thinking—the ability to make judgments and decisions based on evidence and reason—is an essential skill for students in an academic setting, where they're expected to reflect on and analyze information rather than simply remember it. Students need to be prepared to think critically while listening, reading, writing, and participating in discussions. The skills of critical thinking do not develop on their own; they need to be taught, learned, and practiced.

The ability to think critically is also required in most careers, and critical thinking contributes to language acquisition by requiring deep processing of the language. In order to consider an idea in relation to other ideas and then articulate a response or an opinion about it, we must make complex associations in the brain. This in turn leads to better comprehension and retention of the target language.

Here are just a few examples of the academic tasks that require critical thinking skills:

- deciding which material from a lecture to take notes on
- determining a speaker's purpose when assessing the content of a talk
- forming an opinion on an issue based on facts and evidence
- relating new information to one's personal experiences
- giving specific examples to support one's main idea
- assessing the credibility of a source of information

The *Pathways* series gives explicit instruction on and practice of critical thinking skills. Each unit has a Critical Thinking Focus and several practice exercises. For example:

Critical Thinking Focus: Drawing Conclusions

When you draw a conclusion, you make a logical judgment about something based on the information you have. For example, *I might stop by your house. If there are no lights on, and when I knock on the door nobody answers, I'll probably conclude that nobody is home. I can't know this for certain since I can't go into the house and look around, but I do have enough information to reach a logical conclusion.*

 A | In a group, discuss the information from this unit about Angkor and the Khmer Empire and list some conclusions you can draw based on this information. Consider the topics below.

- The length of time that Angkor was the capital of the Khmer Empire
- The art and architecture that can be seen at Angkor
- The number of temples built at Angkor
- The size and sophistication of the water control systems in and around Angkor

> We can conclude that there were a lot of workers in Angkor. Somebody had to construct those huge man-made lakes.

- The fact that Angkor's wealth and power declined after losing river access to the sea
- The fact that Angkor Wat is on UNESCO's World Heritage site list

Teaching with *Pathways Listening, Speaking, and Critical Thinking*

Using the Opening Pages

Each unit of *Pathways Listening, Speaking, and Critical Thinking* begins with a unit opener and a two-page section called Exploring the Theme. These opening pages serve the important function of raising student interest in the unit theme and introducing key vocabulary and concepts.

The Unit Opener

Every unit opener features a stunning photograph that draws students into the unit theme. You'll want to direct students' attention to the photograph and the unit title. Give students a chance to react to the photograph and give the class some of the background information that you'll find in the Teacher's Guide.

Every unit opener also includes Think and Discuss questions that encourage students to interact with the photograph and to relate it to their own lives.

The unit opener also lists the Academic Pathways for each unit. These are clearly stated performance objectives that preview some of the main culminating activities in the unit. The Academic Pathways are also useful in assessing students' progress at the end of each unit.

Exploring the Theme

After you've worked with the unit opener, go on to the two-page Exploring the Theme section, which provides information in the form of maps, captioned photographs, charts and graphs, and short articles. This section gives students the background information and key terms they need before beginning the unit.

The Exploring the Theme questions check students' comprehension of the information and give them a chance to respond to it in a meaningful way.

Building Vocabulary

Each level of *Pathways Listening, Speaking, and Critical Thinking* contains approximately 200 target vocabulary words in addition to footnotes for less frequently used words. The target vocabulary words in the *Pathways* series are . . .

- **High-frequency:** Students are likely to use high-frequency words on a regular basis, which leads to greater acquisition and better fluency.

- **Level-appropriate:** The target vocabulary words in each level of the *Pathways* series are appropriate for the students studying in that level.

- **Useful for discussing the unit theme:** The vocabulary words in each unit are introduced in the vocabulary sections, used in the listening passages, and recycled in many of the activities.

- **Informed by the Academic Word List:** The *Pathways* series contains a high percentage of the words found on the Academic Word List.*

*The Academic Word List (AWL) is a list of the 570 highest-frequency academic word families that regularly appear in academic texts. The AWL was compiled by researcher Averil Coxhead based on her analysis of a 3.5-million-word corpus (Coxhead, 2000).

Developing Listening Skills

Each unit of *Pathways Listening, Speaking, and Critical Thinking* contains two listening sections. The listening passage in Lesson A takes place in a relatively formal context such as a lecture, a meeting, or a formal presentation. Lesson B presents an informal speaking situation such as a conversation between friends or a group project with classmates.

The language in the listening passages represents realistic situations, yet the language is controlled for level, and students may listen to each passage more than once. This guided listening gives students the chance to practice listening and note-taking skills and to develop the confidence and fluency they'll need before they are immersed in an academic setting.

Each listening section contains three parts:

- **Before Listening** activities provide background information and explicit instruction in listening skills.
- **While Listening** activities give students practice in listening for main ideas and smaller details and in making inferences.
- **After Listening** activities are designed to reinforce listening skills and to allow students to discuss and react to the listening passage.

Pronunciation

The pronunciation lessons are designed to increase students' listening comprehension as well as the comprehensibility of their own speech. The focus is on supra-segmentals, such as rhythm and intonation patterns, rather than on individual sounds.

Note-Taking

Pathways Listening, Speaking, and Critical Thinking takes a scaffolding approach to building note-taking skills. Students begin by listening for specific information to fill in blanks. Later they complete partial notes and practice independent note-taking.

Listening Critically

Since critical thinking is an essential part of listening, skills such as identifying a speaker's purpose and summarizing the main points from a talk are part of the *Pathways* listening program.

Listening Homework

Extensive listening can play an important role in increasing listening comprehension. Students can expand on the listening they do in class by using the Audio CD, the Online Workbook, and the Presentation Tool CD-ROM.

Developing Speaking Skills

Every section of *Pathways Listening, Speaking, and Critical Thinking* provides opportunities for classroom speaking and discussion, often in pairs or in small groups. The Exploring Spoken English sections focus entirely on speaking. Striking images and brief stories about real people and places often provide the content for engaging interactions.

Accurate Speech

Clear and succinct grammar lessons give students a single language structure to concentrate on for each Exploring Spoken English section. The grammar points lend themselves to discussion of the unit theme and can be recycled throughout the unit.

Fluent Speech

Frequent classroom discussions and interactions prepare students to participate in class and succeed in an academic setting. Language Function boxes address the situations in which stock expressions or target grammatical structures are commonly used, increasing the students' level of comfort and confidence in dealing with common speaking situations.

Speaking activities are designed with a scaffolding approach. They progress from controlled activities and guided activities to free activities. Early confidence-building motivates students to attempt activities that increase in difficulty, taking them to their ultimate goal—participation in authentic speaking activities such as classroom presentations, formal discussions, and debates.

Presentation Skills boxes appear at points where students give presentations, so they provide immediate practice of skills needed for planning and delivering successful oral presentations.

Student to Student boxes provide tips and expressions to help students develop the informal, one-on-one speaking skills they will need for class work and in their day-to-day exchanges.

Engage is a consolidating speaking activity. It is a task or project involving collaboration with a partner or a group as well as an oral presentation of results or ideas.

Using Videos in the Language Classroom

The video clips in *Pathways Listening, Speaking, and Critical Thinking* come from the award-winning *National Geographic* film collection and act as a bridge between Lesson A and Lesson B of each unit. The videos consolidate content and skills from Lesson A and illustrate a specific aspect of the unit theme in a visually dynamic way.

What is the Lesson A and B Viewing section?

The viewing section features a video on a theme related to the whole unit. All video clips are on the Online Workbook and the Presentation Tool CD-ROM, as well as on the classroom DVD.

Why teach video-viewing skills?

In daily life, non-fiction videos can be found on television, on the Internet, and in movie theaters in the form of documentaries. Just as *Pathways* provides a wide variety of listening passages to build students' listening skills, the series also builds viewing skills with videos from *National Geographic*. *Pathways* promotes visual and digital literacy so learners can competently use a wide range of modern media.

Videos differ from listening texts in important ways. First, students are processing information by viewing and listening simultaneously. Visual images include information about the video's setting as well as clues found in non-verbal communication, such as facial expressions and body movements. The video may also include animated maps and diagrams to explain information and processes. The soundtrack contains narration, conversations, music, and sound effects. Some contextual words may appear on screen in signs or as identification of people or settings. In addition, full English subtitles (closed captions) are available as a teaching and learning option.

What are the stages of viewing?

Before Viewing prepares students for the video, engages their background knowledge about the topic, and creates interest in what they will watch. Effective ways of previewing include:

- brainstorming ideas and discussing what the class already knows about the topic;
- using photographs and the video's title to predict the content;
- pre-teaching key vocabulary essential to understanding the video content;
- and skimming the summary reading.

While Viewing may occur multiple times and at different speeds while:

- picking out and understanding the main ideas of the video;

- watching and listening closely for detail;

- and watching and listening for opinion and inference.

After Viewing activities include:

- describing the main points and the sequence of events in the video;

- completing the cloze summary with provided target vocabulary;

- and answering discussion questions that relate the video to the students' own lives or experiences.

How should teachers use the videos to teach?

The narration on each video has been carefully graded to feature vocabulary items and structures that are appropriate for students' proficiency level. Here are techniques for using video in class:

- Have students preview the video by reading the transcript or the summary paragraph.

- Pause, rewind, or fast-forward the video to focus on key segments or events.

- Pause the video midway to allow students to predict what will happen next. Resume the video so students can check their predictions.

- Have students watch the video with the sound off so they can focus on what they see. If this approach is used, follow-up discussion helps students share their ideas about the content of the video. Then play the video with the sound on for students to check their ideas.

- Have students watch without subtitles after which they discuss what they hear; then play with subtitles for students to check their ideas.

- Have students follow the script as they listen to the video to help with intonation, pitch, and stress. Stop and replay key phrases for students to repeat.

- Have students watch the video independently and complete the comprehension questions on the Online Workbook.

- To extend viewing skills to speaking and writing skills, have students make a presentation or create a written report about a short video of their choice, using language they have learned from the Student Book and video narration.

All video scripts are printed at the back of the Teacher's Guide. Teachers have flexibility in how or whether they want students to use the scripts. See individual units in this Teacher's Guide for specific teaching suggestions for each video.

Features of the *Pathways* Teacher's Guide

The *Pathways* Teacher's Guide contains teaching notes, answer keys, and the audio and video scripts. There are also warm-up activities to help teachers present the material in the textbook and overviews of the unit theme and the video clip to help turn teachers into "instant experts."

Academic Pathways Boxes

Each unit in the Teacher's Guide begins with a preview of the Academic Pathways. A description of each pathway is then given at the point where it occurs in the unit along with helpful information for the teacher. Teachers are also directed to the online and the Assessment CD-ROM with Exam*View®* resources that will help to reinforce and assess the skills learned for each pathway.

Ideas for... Boxes

Throughout the *Pathways* Teacher's Guide, you will find boxes with ideas to help both novice and experienced teachers. There are four types of Ideas for... boxes:

- **Ideas for Presenting Grammar** boxes provide a variety of ways to introduce grammatical structures and utilize the grammar charts.

- **Ideas for Checking Comprehension** boxes remind teachers of the need to continually assess students' comprehension during every class session.

- **Ideas for Expansion** boxes suggest ways to expand on the content of the book when students need extra instruction or when they have a high level of interest in a topic.

- **Ideas for Multi-level Classes** boxes provide techniques to use in mixed-ability classrooms, where learner diversity can benefit everyone in the class. On the other hand, providing the right kind of help for all the students in any classroom can be a balancing act. When different types of instruction are needed for different learners, teachers must be careful not to embarrass lower-level learners in any way or detract from the learning experience of higher-level learners.

Tips

Tips for instruction and classroom management are provided throughout the *Pathways* Teacher's Guide. The tips are especially helpful to less-experienced teachers, but they are also a resource for more experienced teachers, providing new ideas and adding variety to the classroom routine.

Living for Work

Academic Track
Interdisciplinary

Academic Pathways:
Lesson A: Listening to an Interview
Doing an Interview
Lesson B: Listening to an Informal Conversation
Giving a Short Presentation
about Yourself

Unit Theme

When it comes to jobs and careers, some people "work to live"—doing what is necessary to keep themselves and their families alive—while other people "live to work." For those lucky people, employment is a way to do what they enjoy.

Unit 1 explores the topic of work as it relates to:
– adventurous jobs
– career aptitude
– educational requirements
– job duties and benefits
– activities and schedules

 Think and Discuss *(page 1)*

5 mins

Some people love to work outdoors, and doing dangerous work such as high-rise building construction doesn't bother them at all. Other people love to teach, manage a business, or take care of children.

- Point out the unit title and the Academic Pathways at the top of the page. These items will give students a preview of the unit.

- Direct students' attention to the photo and ask where the man might be and what kind of work he is doing.

- Discuss the questions.

> **TIP** Many of the photos in the *Pathways* series have informative captions. There are many ways to use the photos in the *Pathways* series. Discussing the photos in this series is a good way to introduce students to the theme or content of the unit. You might ask students to describe what they see in a photo, for example, or how a photo makes them feel.

Exploring the Theme: Living for Work *(pages 2-3)*

15 mins

The photos and captions in this opening spread present six different jobs as well as useful vocabulary. The map activity introduces students to the international focus of the *Pathways* series.

- Have students read about the six jobs individually or in pairs and then match the photos to the world map.

- Check students' knowledge of the English names for countries and continents as you go over the answers.

- Discuss the questions in the Exploring the Theme box.

Answer Key

Maps should be labeled as follows:
page 2 (from top to bottom): b, a, d
page 3 (from top to bottom): f, e, c

Building and Using Vocabulary *(pages 4-5)*

30 mins

WARM-UP

To introduce the topic of professional photography, show the class example photographs from a magazine with large, color photos.

- As a class, list places where we often see photographs, such as advertisements and newspapers.

- Discuss professional photography. For example:
  - **T:** How much money do you think a photographer makes?
  - **S:** I'm not sure, but it might be different for every photographer.
  - **T:** That's probably true. What words can you think of to describe this kind of work?
  - **S:** Creative, exciting.

Building Vocabulary

track 1-2
Exercise A. | Using a Dictionary

- Play the audio so that students can hear the pronunciation of the five vocabulary words.

- Ask students to take out their dictionaries. Have students look up the vocabulary words and match them to the definitions.

- Have students read pages 208 and 209 of the *Independent Student Handbook* for some information about building vocabulary skills. Encourage students to start a vocabulary journal according to the suggestions mentioned in the handbook.

Answer Key   1. c 2. a 3. d 4. e 5. b

track 1-3
Exercise B. | Meaning from Context
Have students read the article as they listen to the audio. Have them focus on the five additional vocabulary words presented in the article.

Exercise C.

- Encourage students to do the exercise using context clues from the article in exercise **B**.

- As you go over the answers, help students identify the context clues that helped them choose the correct word for each definition.

Answer Key   1. creative 2. explore 3. adventure 4. communicate 5. help

Exercise D. | Using a Dictionary   Explain to students that dictionaries give information beyond the definition of words. The focus of exercise **D** is on word families and parts of speech.

TIP   To help students understand the concept of different parts of speech, write an example sentence for each of the first three words in exercise D: *Exploration is a way to learn about new places. We can explore new places on foot. It was an exploratory trip.*

Answer Key

Noun	Verb	Adjective
exploration	explore	exploratory
communication	communicate	communicative
help	help	helpful
creativity	create	creative

Using Vocabulary

Exercise A. | Have pairs of students fill in the blanks to complete the conversation. Then tell pairs to practice the conversation.

Answer Key   1. opportunity 2. creative 3. explore 4. communicate 5. help

track 1-4
Exercise B. | Annie Griffiths is a well-known professional photographer. This exercise introduces her to students as they put vocabulary words in context.

Answer Key   1. travel 2. adventure 3. experiences 4. dangerous 5. skills

Developing Listening Skills
(pages 6-7)

45 mins

Before Listening

Predicting Content | Tell students that the interview in this section is with Annie Griffiths, the photographer who was introduced in the Using Vocabulary section on page 5. Have students activate their prior knowledge by predicting what the interview will be about. Have them discuss their ideas with their partner.

Listening: An Interview

Critical Thinking Focus: Identifying Main Ideas | Go over the information in the box. Explain to students that distinguishing main ideas from details is an essential critical thinking skill. Remind students that the main idea applies to the whole listening passage. Each detail is only about a smaller part of the passage.

Exercise A. | Listening for Main Ideas

track 1-5

■ Play the audio. Have students listen and choose the main idea of the interview.

Answer Key

✓ Annie Griffiths's job as a photographer is very interesting.

IDEAS FOR... **Checking Comprehension**

Call on students to explain why the other two statements in exercise **A** are NOT the main idea of the interview. Make sure they understand that the statements are true, but they are only a small part of the whole interview.

Exercise B. | Listening for Details   Give students time to read the questions and answer choices before they listen to the interview again.

track 1-5

Answer Key   1. c 2. a 3. a 4. b 5. b

After Listening

Exercise A. | Making Inferences   As you go over the answers, ask students to explain their choices. (Possible explanations are included in the Answer Key box below.) Explaining their choices will require students to recall specific parts of the listening passage.

Answer Key

1. T (She uses words such as "like," "love," and "enjoy.")
2. T (She explains how she does it.)
3. F (The interviewer says that "her work takes her to dangerous places" and places where there is war.)
4. F (She says they "loved" some of the places and had fun.)

Exercise B. | Self-Reflection   Have students discuss the questions in pairs. Encourage them to give their personal opinions about some of the topics from the listening passage.

TIP   At the beginning of a course, it's important for students to get to know each other and become comfortable speaking English together. Use a variety of ways to assign partners and form small groups so that students are not always working with the same people.

IDEAS FOR... **Expansion**

As partners discuss the questions in exercise **B**, walk around the classroom and take notes on some of their ideas. At the end of the exercise, share those ideas with the whole class to start a class discussion.

TIP   The captions of the four photos on pages 6 and 7 include locations. Ask students to point out those places on pages 2 and 3 or on a world map in the classroom.

Exploring Spoken English

45 mins *(pages 8-10)*

Language Function: Communicating that You Don't Understand

Go over the information in the box. Tell students that it's important for native speakers as well as people learning a language to indicate when they don't understand something a speaker says. These expressions are useful for letting a speaker know when you don't understand what they are saying.

track 1-6 **Exercise A.**

Answer Key

What's that?

I'm not sure what you mean.

Exercise B. | Have partners practice the conversation twice—first taking one speaking role and then the other.

> **TIP** Teach your students to read a line of a conversation, look up from the page, and say the line to their partner. Doing this requires students to process the language in order to remember the line, and making eye contact while speaking is a natural way to role-play a real conversation.

Exercise C. | Have students choose from the expressions in the Language Function box in order to complete the conversations.

Grammar: The Simple Present vs. the Present Continuous

> **IDEAS FOR...** **Presenting Grammar**
>
> Students have almost certainly seen these two verb tenses before. Let them know that this is a review.
>
> ▪ Go over the information in the box. After you read each sentence, call on a student to give you another example using the target tense.
>
> ▪ Write students' sentences on the board as they say them. Ask the class if each sentence is correct.

Exercise A. | At this level, choosing the correct verb may be as challenging for students as choosing the correct tense in this exercise. Encourage students to use their dictionaries or to ask questions about any unfamiliar vocabulary.

Answer Key

1. work 2. am cooking 3. am writing 4. show 5. sell
6. am showing 7. am texting 8. is teaching 9. help

Exercise B. | Have students work in pairs to fill in the blanks.

Answer Key

1. works 2. helps 3. doesn't make 4. is looking
5. is helping 6. are making 7. doesn't have

> **IDEAS FOR...** **Checking Comprehension**
>
> Direct students to some of the other photos in the unit such as the ones on pages 11, 12, and 14. Call on different students and ask them questions that require the simple present or present continuous. For example:
> *What does she do for a living?*
> *What is she doing right now?*
> *Do you think he makes a lot of money?*
> *What is he thinking about right now?*

Exercise C.

▪ Point out the caption of each photo and say the words for occupations. Ask students to repeat after you.

▪ Discuss each occupation briefly as a class. For example:
  T: Where does a chef work?
  S: In a restaurant.
  T: Good. And what does a chef do at a restaurant?
  S: He cooks food.

▪ Have students complete the exercise.

Exercise D. | Discussion

- If students have been working with the same partner, ask them to do exercise **D** with a new partner.
- Call on different pairs of students to tell the class their answers to items 1 and 3.

Speaking

30-45 mins

Doing an Interview (page 11)

WARM-UP

- Direct students' attention to the conversation in exercise **A** on page 8. Ask them what a career aptitude test is.
- Tell students that in this exercise they will take a career aptitude test.

Exercise A. | Note-Taking

- Go over the directions and point out the space in the chart where students can take notes on their partner's answers.
- Ask the class: *Can you write a little or a lot in this space?* Explain that they will only write a few words to help them remember their partner's answers.
- Tell students how much time they have to do the interview (perhaps five minutes for each partner), and encourage them to explain and give reasons for their answers.
- Encourage students to read pages 206 and 207 of the *Independent Student Handbook* for more information about improving note-taking skills.

TIP   Model the interview activity with a volunteer before asking students to complete the task. Ask the volunteer one or two of the questions from the interview and write brief notes on the board. Ask follow-up questions if necessary to encourage the student to give more details.

Exercise B. | Have students work with the same partners they interviewed in exercise **A**.

Exercise C. | Have students report their ideas about their partners' career aptitude to another pair of students, or to the whole class if time permits. Give students a chance to react to their group members' job recommendations.

Viewing: Butler School

30 mins

(pages 12-13)

Overview of the Video | Becoming a professional butler might not be everyone's first career choice. However, in England, the Ivor Spencer School for Butler Administrators prepares its students for this interesting job, which involves everything from selecting the best shoes for employers to ironing their newspapers.

Before Viewing

Exercise A. | Prior Knowledge Have students decide if each statement is true or false based on what they already know about butlers.

> **Answer Key** *(Answers may vary.)*
>
> 1. T 2. T 3. F 4. T

Exercise B. | Using a Dictionary Have students use their dictionaries to complete this exercise.

> **Answer Key**   1. d 2. a 3. b 4. c

While Viewing

 6:14

Exercise A. | Give students time to read the questions and answer choices before you show them the video for the first time.

> **Answer Key**   1. many 2. few 3. many countries 4. difficult

> **TIP** You can show the video with or without captions depending on your goals. Showing the video without captions allows students to concentrate on the images and general ideas and to experience an authentic listening task. Showing the video with captions puts the emphasis on language and creates a reading task.

6:14

Exercise B. | Using the Simple Present

All of the answer choices are phrases in the simple present tense. You can emphasize this and recycle the grammar point as you go over the exercise. For example:

T: Do students graduate from the butler school?

S: Yes, they do.

T: Good. They graduate from the school. And why do we use the simple present in this sentence?

S: It's a repeated action. It probably happens a few times a year.

> **Answer Key**
>
> ✓ graduate from the school
> ✓ iron newspapers
> ✓ learn to walk correctly
> ✓ practice saying things

After Viewing

Exercise A. | Discussion

- Go over the directions. Call on two students to read the speech bubbles aloud, or read them with a student volunteer to model the activity.

- Give students a chance to report on their discussions—either by calling on different pairs to share some of their ideas with the class or by having students change partners and tell their new partners about their discussions.

Exercise B. | Critical Thinking This exercise requires students to perform several tasks, beginning with following the instructions. You may want to walk around the classroom and offer assistance and encouragement while students are working.

Building and Using Vocabulary *(pages 14-15)*

30 mins

WARM-UP

The target vocabulary for Lesson B is presented in the context of three interviews with workers. Point to each picture on page 14 and ask questions. Ask: *What is her/his job? Do you think it's a good job? Why?*

Building Vocabulary

track 1-7

Exercise A. | Meaning from Context Play the audio. Have students listen and read along in the Student Book.

Exercise B. | Using a Dictionary

- Have students check the words they're already familiar with.

- As students look up new words, have them go back to the interviews and read the sentence in which each word is used.

> **IDEAS FOR...** Expansion
>
> - Help students identify some of the context clues that can help them understand the vocabulary words. For example, in the first interview, the nurse gives a good explanation of the word "organized" in her first answer.
> - After you do the vocabulary exercise, use the interviews for speaking practice. Have students practice the interviews in pairs. Then ask for volunteers to role-play one interview for the class.

Using Vocabulary

Exercise A. | Have students fill in the blanks with vocabulary words from the box.

> **Answer Key**
> 1. although 2. search 3. presentations 4. graduate 5. physical 6. effect

Exercise B. | Have students use the vocabulary words in the box to complete the job interview.

> **Answer Key**
> 1. believe 2. graduated 3. organized 4. in charge of 5. Although

Exercise C. | Role-Playing Students ask their partner the questions from the job interview in exercise **B**. The partner who is answering the questions uses his or her own ideas instead of the answers given by Jenny in exercise **B**.

> **TIP** Role-playing is a creative skill that can be very useful in language classes, but it needs to be taught and practiced. Model the exercise first by calling on a student to read the first question from the job interview aloud. Answer the question with new information. For example: *Yes, I do. I love to paint and draw pictures, and I like to be creative at work, too.*

Exercise D. | Critical Thinking Make sure students use the target vocabulary as they think about and respond to the questions.

> **TIP** Every question in exercise D has more than one part. As you walk around the classroom and monitor students, make sure they are taking the time to discuss the questions completely.

Developing Listening Skills

45 mins

(pages 16-17)

track 1-8

Pronunciation: Syllable Stress

Go over the information in the box. Explain to students that syllable number and syllable stress are the basic elements of the rhythm of English. Understanding the pronunciation of syllables can greatly improve language learners' listening comprehension as well as their ability to be understood when they speak.

track 1-9

Exercise A. | Have students listen and underline the syllable with the main stress in each word. Play the audio a second time to allow students to check their answers.

Answer Key

1. <u>nurse</u> 2. <u>study</u> 3. <u>trav</u>el 4. re<u>mem</u>ber 5. re<u>port</u>er
6. cre<u>at</u>ive 7. re<u>ceive</u> 8. <u>skills</u>

track 1-10

Exercise B. | Have students group the words according to syllable number.

Answer Key

One-syllable Words: cook, fly, know

Two-syllable Words: money, teacher, travel

Three-syllable Words: adventure, amazing, officer, yesterday

track 1-11

Before Listening

This exercise checks students' comprehension of syllable pronunciation and presents key vocabulary from the main listening passage. Have students work individually to complete the two items.

Answer Key

<u>bi</u>llion (2), ma<u>rine</u> bi<u>o</u>logist (2, 4), <u>o</u>cean (2), po<u>llu</u>tion (3), <u>tu</u>na (2)

Listening: An Informal Conversation

track 1-12

Exercise A. | Explain to students that they are going to hear the first part of a conversation between two students. Tell them to focus on identifying the topic of the conversation.

Answer Key

✓ a presentation that Becca missed

track 1-13

Exercise B. | Listening for Main Ideas

- Give students time to read the answer choices before they listen.

- Play the audio.

- As you go over the exercise, remind students of the difference between main ideas and details.

Answer Key

✓ Dr. Earle says the world's people are having a bad effect on the oceans.

track 1-13

Exercise C. | Listening for Details As students listen again, they check the details that are not mentioned in the listening.

Answer Key

✓ Dr. Earle earns a high salary.
✓ It's fine to eat tuna and other large ocean fish.

After Listening

Exercise A. | Self-Reflection Ask students to decide whether they agree or disagree with the statements.

Student to Student: Giving Feedback while Listening | Go over the information in the box. Explain to students that the Student to Student boxes provide speaking strategies and useful phrases for interacting in social situations—an important part of academic life.

Exercise B. | Discussion
- Put students into small groups to discuss their answers from exercise **A**.

- Encourage students to use expressions from the Student to Student box for showing interest.

30 mins

Exploring Spoken English
(pages 18-19)

Grammar: Adverbs of Frequency

Exercise A. | The grammar in this lesson is presented using an inductive approach. Have students practice the conversation in pairs so that they will see the target grammar in the context of a conversation.

Exercise B. | Discussion   Have students answer the questions before you present the information in the grammar box.

Answer Key *(Answers may vary.)*

1. Yes. He says he <u>always</u> writes before bed.
2. No. He says Chris <u>sometimes</u> writes during the day.
3. No. He says he <u>seldom</u> sees anyone writing in a journal.

IDEAS FOR...   **Presenting Grammar**

- Go over the explanation and the two example sentences in the top part of the chart.
- Say the list of adverbs and have students repeat each word after you.
- If students ask, explain that most adverbs of frequency don't tell us *exactly* how often things happen. Only the words "always" (100%) and "never" (0%) have a completely clear meaning.
- As you go over the list of example sentences, ask students to identify the verb in each sentence. Then write that verb and the adverb of frequency on the board.
- When you have finished, look back at the rule for the placement of adverbs of frequency. (They go before most verbs, but after the verb *be*.) Point to the list of verbs and adverbs you wrote on the board to illustrate the pattern.

Exercise C. | Have students complete the sentences individually.

Answer Key *(Answers may vary.)*

1. always 2. usually 3. seldom 4. sometimes
5. often 6. occasionally

Exercise D. | Have students compare answers to exercise **C** in pairs. Partners will probably find some differences in their answers. Tell them that the important thing is for their sentences to make logical sense.

Language Function: Using Adverbs of Frequency

Exercise A. | Have students work in pairs to answer the questions. Explain the difference between the word "housekeeper," which refers to a person who cleans homes or hotel rooms as a job, and the words "homemaker" and "housewife," which refer to people who don't work outside of the home, but spend their days taking care of their own families without pay.

Answer Key

1. She works Tuesday through Saturday. She doesn't work on Sunday or Monday.
2. Her longest workday is Thursday (10.5 hours). Her shortest workday is Saturday (5 hours).
3. Erica does all of the job duties listed at the bottom of the schedule. (She cleans the guest bedrooms, makes beds, etc.)

Exercise B. | Direct students' attention to the speech bubbles on this page. Explain that they are examples for this discussion activity.

Exercise C. | Discussion   Have students discuss Erica's job in groups of three or four. The discussion requires students to recycle vocabulary from earlier parts of the unit.

Engage: Giving a Short Presentation about Yourself

45 mins

(page 20)

WARM-UP

The Engage exercise for Unit 1 moves away from the topic of jobs and work, and instead focuses on the students themselves.

- Go over the brief description of the exercise at the top of the page.

- Point out the questionnaire in exercise **A**. Then call on two or three students in the class to answer each of the questions.

- Give students the opportunity to ask you the last two questions from the chart.

Exercise A. | Planning a Presentation

- Give students time to fill out the questionnaire individually.

- Encourage students to tell their partners about their answers—not just show them the answers.

Presentation Skills: Introducing Yourself

Go over the information in the Presentation Skills box. Tell students that introducing oneself is an essential part of most presentations.

Exercise B. | Planning a Presentation

track 1-14

- Play the audio and have students read along in the Student Book.

- Have students follow the directions.

- As you go over the answers, point out the information in item 2 is a detail about Alejandro, and that details help to make a presentation interesting.

Answer Key

1. <u>Hi</u>, <u>My name is</u>
2. I'm from Bogotá . . . that's the capital city of Colombia
3. Answers will vary.

TIP

If you have enough class time, give students a chance to practice their presentations. They do not need to write out every word they plan to say. Instead, have students say their presentations quietly to themselves or to a partner.

Exercise C. | Presentation

- Before students give their presentations in groups or to the whole class, model the activity by introducing yourself.

- There are two main goals of this presentation. The first is to let students in the class get to know each other better. The second is to begin the process of getting comfortable with giving presentations in English.

TIP

The task itself is fairly simple, but nervousness can be a very real problem at the beginning of the course, and especially when speaking a language that is not one's native language. Try to keep the classroom atmosphere light and enjoyable for this activity.

Good Times, Good Feelings

Academic Track
**Psychology/
Sociology**

Academic Pathways:
Lesson A: Listening to a Lecture
           Discussing Celebrations and Holidays
Lesson B: Listening to a Talk with Questions
           and Answers
           Giving a Presentation for a Small Group

Unit Theme

Unit 2 is about fun, laughter, holidays, celebrations, and leisure time. It's about having good times with other people and feeling good about ourselves.

Unit 2 explores the topic of good times and good feelings as it relates to:
– the origin of laughter   – leisure time and activities
– when and why people laugh   – the value of public parks
– ways in which we celebrate

 # Think and Discuss *(page 21)*

**5
mins**

The fields of psychology and sociology search for universal truths about human beings. Feelings of happiness and the need to share those feelings with friends, family, and other social groups are universal human emotions.

- Point out the unit title and the Academic Pathways at the top of the page. These items will give students a preview of the unit.

- Discuss the Think and Discuss questions.

- Encourage students to comment on the photo. For example:

  T: Look at this man. Do you sometimes feel this way?
  S: Yes, sometimes.
  T: When you feel this way, what are you doing?
  S: I'm sitting on the beach on a warm, sunny day, or maybe playing volleyball with my friends.

Exploring the Theme: Good Times, Good Feelings
(pages 22-23)

**15
mins**

The opening spread features a striking photograph from a hot air balloon festival in the United States. A hot air balloon uses a gas burner to heat the air inside the balloon so it can lift its passenger basket into the air. It's not a very practical form of transportation, but it is fun, and the balloons themselves are symbols of the unit's theme: sunshine, flowers, smiling faces, and a snowman.

- Have students look at the photos and read the captions.

- Discuss the questions.

> **TIP** As students answer question #3, list their favorite activities and why they like them on the board. Write down only key words to model note-taking.

Building and Using Vocabulary *(pages 24-25)*

30 mins

WARM-UP

The Lesson A vocabulary is presented in the context of research findings about the possible origin of human laughter.

- Have students look at the picture of the chimpanzee on page 24.

- Remind students of the unit theme and ask: *Why is this chimp in a unit on good times and good feelings?*

- Students may say that the chimp is smiling or that seeing animals makes people happy. Respond with interest to students' ideas.

Building Vocabulary

 Exercise A.
track 1-15

- Give students time to look over the list and check the words they are familiar with.

- Play the audio so that students can hear the pronunciation of each word.

Exercises B and C.
track 1-16

- Play the audio and ask students to read along in the Student Book.

- Give students time to match each word in blue with its definition in exercise **C**. Encourage them to try the exercise using context clues instead of a dictionary.

- As you go over the answers, help students identify some of the context clues from the reading.

Answer Key

1. funny	5. joy	9. laughter
2. unique	6. led	10. situations
3. noise	7. joke	
4. researchers	8. recorded	

Using Vocabulary

Exercise A. | Have students use the vocabulary words found in the reading on page 24 to complete the dialogs.

Answer Key

1. situations 2. joy 3. led 4. researchers 5. unique
6. joke, funny 7. laughter 8. recorded 9. noise

IDEAS FOR... Multi-level Classes

The students themselves can be very helpful in classes with mixed abilities, but only if they are willing to work with each other. Try using the "rotating lines" technique after students finish exercise **A**—both as fluency practice and as a tool to get students used to talking with every member of the class.

- Have students form two lines. Each student stands facing another student. (For a large class, you may need more than two lines.)

- Students practice item 1 in exercise **A** twice, alternating roles so that every student says every sentence.

- Then one line of students moves to the left so that everyone has a new partner. The student on the far left walks to the far right of the line.

- Repeat the procedure with the next exchange in exercise **A** until all the students in one line have interacted with all of the students in the other line.

Exercise B. | Self-Reflection Have students discuss the questions about laughter and humor in groups of three or four.

TIP Ask for one volunteer from each group to read the discussion questions aloud and make sure everyone in the group speaks during the discussion.

Developing Listening Skills

45 mins

(pages 26-27)

Before Listening

Exercise A. | Discussion Have students discuss the questions about the two photos in pairs. Students might predict that the women in the second photo are more likely to laugh. In fact, students will learn in the listening passage that people usually do not laugh when they're alone.

Exercise B. | Predicting Content

- Have partners predict which topics they might hear about in a lecture on laughter.

- As you go over students' predictions, ask them why they think or do not think each topic might be in the lecture.

- Ask students if they have additional ideas about possible lecture topics.

Listening: A Lecture

Critical Thinking Focus: Understanding the Speaker's Purpose | Go over the information in the box. Explain to students that thinking critically while listening involves a complex set of analytical skills. Considering a speaker's purpose is one way to gain a perspective on someone's words.

track 1-17 **Exercise A. | Understanding the Speaker's Purpose** Have students listen to an excerpt from the main listening passage to determine the speaker's purpose.

Answer Key   1. b 2. b

track 1-18 **Exercise B. | Checking Predictions** Play the audio again so that students can listen to the main listening passage and check their predictions from exercise **B** on page 26.

TIP After you play the audio, point to exercise B in the Before Listening section on page 26 and ask the class about each topic. For example: *Did the speaker talk about reasons people laugh?*

track 1-18 **Exercise C. | Listening for Main Ideas**

- Give students time to read the questions and answer choices.

- Play the audio a second time. Have students choose the correct answers.

Answer Key   1. c 2. a 3. c

track 1-18 **Exercise D. | Listening for Details**
After students have read the statements, play the audio again. Have students complete the statements with specific information from the listening.

Answer Key   1. Bowling Green 2. high
3. 80 4. laugh

After Listening

Critical Thinking | Have students discuss the questions in pairs. Encourage them to go beyond the information from the unit and the listening passage and to use their own observations of the world to form and explain their opinions.

IDEAS FOR...   Expansion

Ask students to bring to class an example of something they think is funny, such as a picture, a comic strip from a newspaper, a movie on DVD, or a funny story or joke they can tell. Explain that you want examples of "clean" humor that will not upset anyone.

Have small groups share and discuss the humorous examples they bring to class. Have students try to explain why their example is funny to them.

Exploring Spoken English

45 mins

(pages 28-30)

Language Function: Asking Questions to Show Interest

For someone learning a new language, knowing how to respond to something a person says can be confusing. There are many possible ways to respond with interest. The information in this box gives students a few useful expressions.

Exercise A. | Have students look for clues in the first speaker's sentence that indicate how the second speaker might respond.

> **TIP** Have students use each expression from the box only once. The process of elimination may be helpful in choosing an appropriate expression.

Answer Key *(Answers may vary.)*

1. Oh, why? 2. Good for you! 3. Really? 4. How funny? 5. Oh, that's too bad.

Exercises B and C. | Have students practice the conversations from exercise **A** in pairs. Then have partners make up conversations about what makes them laugh. Make sure they use the new expressions for showing interest.

Grammar: The Simple Present Tense—*Yes/No* Questions

> **IDEAS FOR...** **Presenting Grammar**
>
> Give students some practice forming *yes/no* questions in the simple present.
>
> - Prepare a list of statements about your family members or other people. For example:
>   *My wife/husband enjoys funny movies.*
>   *Our children think everything is funny.*
> - Say each sentence to the class. Then call on one student to change the sentence into a *yes/no* question.
> - Give students a chance to ask you their own *yes/no* questions.

Exercise A. | Have students complete the *yes/no* questions in the survey about happiness.

Answer Key

2. Do, do 3. Do, have 4. Do, take 5. Are 6. Are 7. Do, keep 8. Do, like

Exercise B. | Have students complete the survey individually.

Exercise C. | Discussion Ask students to share answers with their partners. Encourage them to discuss the significance of the survey as well.

Pronunciation: The Intonation of *Yes/No* Questions

track 1-19

Play the audio so that students can hear the examples in the pronunciation box.

track 1-20

Exercise A. | In these examples, the speaker's voice rises on the last word in each question. In real life, intonation isn't always so neat, but the rising intonation should begin on the last content word in a *yes/no* question.

- Have students underline the words where the speaker's voice rises.

Answer Key

1. lot 2. weddings 3. sitcoms 4. parties

Exercise B. | Students often under-emphasize English intonation patterns. Encourage them to exaggerate the question intonation as they practice these conversations.

Exercise C. | Have students use the prompts to ask each other *yes/no* questions. Students can use this as a simple substitution activity by changing parts of the example conversation. They can also improvise conversations using their own ideas.

Exercise D. | Go over the directions. Model the activity. Call on three students to read the roles of A, B, and C in the box. Set a time limit for small groups to do the activity.

Speaking: Discussing Celebrations and Holidays

30-45 mins

(page 31)

WARM-UP

Write the names of several holidays and celebrations on the board. These might be popular in the country where you are teaching, or they might represent the countries students are from. Some examples include *New Year's Eve, birthday parties, Independence Day, weddings, Thanksgiving, graduation parties,* etc. Lead a class discussion and recycle *yes/no* questions. Ask students whether they celebrate these occasions and what they do to celebrate them.

Exercise A. | **Self-Reflection**   Have students fill in the column of the chart labeled *My Answers*. Tell students that brief notes are acceptable for this exercise.

Exercise B. | Ask partners to use the chart to interview each other, showing interest and asking follow-up questions. Again, students only need to write brief notes on their partner's answers.

Exercise C.

- Have each pair of students join another pair of students to form a group of four.

- In the new groups of four, have each person talk about his or her partner.

- Encourage students to continue to show interest and ask follow-up questions.

TIP   If you don't have an even number of students in the class for pair work, you can act as a partner yourself and work with one student, or you can ask two students to work together on the same holiday or celebration. In the exercises on this page, for example, two students could agree on a holiday or celebration and fill in the column of the chart labeled *My Answers* together.

IDEAS FOR...   Expansion

Speaking to the whole class is a helpful way for students to overcome nervousness about public speaking.

- Ask each group to agree on one very interesting thing from their discussion and one very surprising thing. Call on students at random to report to the class on one of these things.

- Students will do a presentation on a favorite holiday, celebration, or leisure activity in the Engage exercise on page 40, so you may not wish to have students give an in-depth presentation at this point.

Viewing: Nubian Wedding

30-45 mins

(pages 32-33)

Overview of the Video | In many cultures, weddings are happy occasions—often full of rituals and traditions. In the Nubian culture, the celebration goes on for days. Even though the Nubian population was forced from its homeland in Egypt when the Aswan Dam was built, traditional wedding rituals live on—along with a few modern additions.

Before Viewing

Exercise A. | Prior Knowledge   Have students choose the celebrations that they like individually before they discuss their reasons with their partners.

Exercise B. | Understanding Maps   Explain to students that the maps on this page will prepare them for what they will see in the video.

Answer Key	1. northern or northeastern
	2. Egypt, Sudan

Exercise C. | Using a Dictionary

- Go over the directions. Explain that the Nubian culture is an ethnic group, and that most Nubian people are Muslims, meaning that they practice the religion of Islam.

- Give students time to read the text and use their dictionaries.

- Go over the underlined words and check students' comprehension.

Exercise D. | Have students ask and answer the questions with a partner. The target grammar of Lesson B is introduced: *wh-* questions in the simple present.

While Viewing

Exercise A.

3:38

- Give students time to read the questions.

- Play the video without the captions so that students need to listen for (rather than read) the information they need.

Answer Key

1. seven days and nights **2.** the entire village **3.** in front of the groom's house **4.** after midnight **5.** a white wedding dress

Exercise B.

3:38

- Give students time to read the statements.

- Play the video again—with or without the captions.

- As you go over the answers, ask students to make corrections so that the false statements are true.

Answer Key

1. F (Life changed for the Nubian people in the 1960s.)
2. T **3.** T **4.** F (He thinks life was better before.) **5.** T

After Viewing

Critical Thinking | Have students form small groups to discuss the questions. While discussing the questions, students will do several critical thinking tasks, including giving a personal reaction, making comparisons, and identifying the main purpose of the video.

TIP   Use a variety of ways to form pairs and small groups so that students are not always working with the same people. For example, divide the class into six groups by having students count off to six and asking students to form a group with other people who have the same number. Another way to divide the class is to form six groups by birth month. Everyone born in January or February is in the first group, everyone born in March and April is in the second group, and so on.

30 mins

Building and Using Vocabulary *(pages 34-35)*

WARM-UP

The Lesson B target vocabulary is presented in the context of statements from four different speakers about leisure time.

- Ask students about their favorite things to do after class or on weekends.

- Ask students to estimate how many hours of free time they have (when they're not working and not studying) in a normal day or normal week.

Building Vocabulary

track 1-21

Exercise A. | Meaning from Context

- Point to the four photos and tell students that they will hear these people talk about their free time.

- Ask the class to come up with a name for each person in the photos. Write the names on the board. This will engage students in the activity and make it easier to discuss each person's information.

- Play the audio and have students read along in the Student Book.

Exercise B. | Have students match the vocabulary words to their definitions using clues in the speakers' statements.

| **Answer Key** | 1. d 2. g 3. e 4. b 5. c |
| | 6. j 7. i 8. a 9. f 10. h |

IDEAS FOR... Checking Comprehension

After students complete exercise **B**, go back to each paragraph and call on students to point out the context clues near each vocabulary word. For example: *The first speaker doesn't have much* free time *because of his* full-time *job. He works a lot, so* free time *must be time when he's not working.*

Using Vocabulary

Exercise A. | This exercise requires students to use the vocabulary words in the context of an article about city parks, which is also the topic of the main listening passage in Lesson B.

- Have students read the article and fill in each blank with a vocabulary word.

- Briefly discuss the article as you go over the answers to exercise **A**.

- Give students a chance to ask any questions they have.

- Ask students about the benefits of city parks.

Answer Key

1. free time	5. relax	9. common
2. enjoy	6. exercise	10. together
3. drawback	7. outdoors	
4. benefits	8. healthy	

> **TIP** Point out that the article only mentions one drawback (the cost). Ask students why the cost is a drawback (e.g., money the city spends on parks becomes unavailable for other things such as housing or police).

Exercise B. | Critical Thinking Have students discuss the questions in pairs.

> **TIP** Ask students to list the ideas they come up with in exercise **B**. Writing their ideas down will give a focus to their discussion as well as an end product.

Developing Listening Skills

45 mins

(pages 36-37)

Before Listening

Predicting Content | In preparation for the listening passage, partners discuss a question about what the speaker might say.

> **TIP** The photo on page 36 is of New York City's Central Park, one of the best-known city parks in the world. Ask students if they've ever been to Central Park or seen it in movies or on television.

Listening: A Talk with Questions and Answers

Depending on students' culture and personality, asking questions in class may be quite easy or be practically unthinkable. The Lesson B listening passage involves a guest speaker giving a fairly informal talk, and it provides a model for an interactive classroom exchange.

Exercise A. | Listening for Main Ideas

track 1-22

- Give students time to read the statements.
- Play the audio. Pause the audio to allow students to fill in the blanks.

> **Answer Key** 1. benefits 2. health 3. crime 4. problems

Exercise B. | Listening for Details

track 1-22

- Give students time to read the statements.
- Play the audio a second time as students listen and choose the correct answers.

> **Answer Key** 1. b 2. a 3. b

After Listening

Exercise A. | Ranking Information

Ask students to work individually to rank the benefits according to their own ideas.

Exercise B. | Giving Opinions Have partners discuss their rankings from exercise **A** and their reasons.

Pronunciation: The Intonation of *Wh-* Questions

track 1-23

In Lesson A, students learned about the formation and intonation of *yes/no* questions. In Lesson B, the focus is on *wh-* questions, also called information questions because they require more than a simple "yes" or "no" for the answer.

- Go over the information in the box.
- Play the audio so that students can hear the examples.

Exercise A.

track 1-24

- Have students work individually to predict the intonation patterns.
- Play the audio as students check the predictions they made.

> **Answer Key**
>
> Where is it?
> Why do people go there?
> What do you do in your free time?
> Why do you do that?
> When are you going next?

> **TIP** Stop the audio after the first conversation to answer any questions about *wh-* question intonation.

Exercise B. | Have students use *wh-* question intonation as they practice the conversations in pairs.

Exploring Spoken English
(pages 38-39)

30 mins

Language Function: Making Small Talk

Go over the information in the box. Explain to students that small talk is not common in every culture, but English speakers use it fairly often. Giving students some guidelines and practice with small talk allows them to participate in this socially important form of talk about everyday topics.

track 1-25

Exercise A. | Have students listen to and read a conversation that takes place at a public park. As they listen, ask them to underline examples of small talk.

Answer Key

What's the temperature today?

Exercise B. | Have students practice the conversation from exercise **A** in pairs.

Grammar: The Simple Present Tense—*Wh-* Questions

> ·IDEAS FOR...   **Presenting Grammar**
>
> With *wh-* questions, a common learner error is to place the *wh-* question word at the beginning of a statement without changing the statement in any other way. For example:
> *Why <u>the store is</u> closed today?* (incorrect)
> *Why <u>is the store</u> closed today?* (correct)
>
> ■ Before you go over the information in the grammar box, review *yes/no* questions from Lesson A.
>
> ■ Remind students that questions with *be* require a change in word order (verb first, then subject), and that questions with other verbs require the auxiliary verb *do*.
>
> ■ Write several sentences in the simple present on the board and call on students to form *yes/no* questions from the statements.

Exercise A. | Have students work individually to complete the *wh-* questions.

Answer Key

2. What is 3. Who do you send 4. How do you relax
5. Where is 6. Why are

Exercise B. | Have partners ask one another the questions in exercise A and answer with their own ideas.

Exercise C. | Discussion   Have students talk about the suggested topics. Encourage their partners to ask wh- questions to show interest.

TIP   To encourage fluency, set a time limit for each round of discussion in exercise C (for example, one or two minutes for each topic). Tell students when to start talking and tell them to stop when their time is up.

track 1-26 **Exercise D.**

■ Go over the information about asking for repetition in the Student to Student box.

■ Play the audio and then have students practice the conversation in pairs.

Exercise E.

■ Go over the directions and model the example conversation. Ask a student to volunteer to play Partner B.

■ Partners have mini-conversations using the prompts. Partner A says something indistinctly, and Partner B asks for repetition.

Engage: Giving a Presentation for a Small Group *(page 40)*

45 mins

WARM-UP

The Engage activity for Unit 2 continues the unit themes of good times and good feelings.

- Go over the brief description of the activity at the top of the page.

- Make a simple chart with three columns on the board. Label the columns *holidays*, *celebrations*, and *free time activities*.

- For each column, call on several students in the class to give you an example that they enjoy. Ask, for example: *Mina, what holiday do you enjoy?*

- Continue until you have several examples in each column on the board.

Exercise A. | Brainstorming Have students think about and write down three or four possible topics for their presentation.

Exercise B. | Planning a Presentation

- Go over the directions with the class.

- Go over the sample notes. Explain that presentation notes should be large enough and brief enough to be helpful when you look at them quickly during a presentation.

- Point out the three parts of the presentation:
  (1) the *introduction*, which gives the main idea;
  (2) the *body*, which gives specific details; and
  (3) the *conclusion*, which tells the audience why the topic is important.

- Tell students how much time they will have for their presentation—approximately two to three minutes per person.

> **TIP** If you have enough class time, give students a chance to practice their presentations, either quietly to themselves or with a partner.

Exercise C. | Presentation

- Go over the information in the Presentation Skills box.

- Divide the class into small groups of three to four students.

- Go over the steps and make sure students understand the procedure.

> **IDEAS FOR... Expansion**
>
> Direct students to the *Independent Student Handbook* at the back of the Student Book to reinforce the information on the Engage page. For example:
>
> - pages 202–203: Understanding the Structure of a Presentation
> - page 212: Speaking Clearly and Comprehensibly
>
> Encourage students to consult this resource throughout the course.

Treasures from the Past

Academic Track
History/Archaeology

Academic Pathways:
Lesson A: Listening to a Talk about an
Ancient City
Talking about the Past

Lesson B: Listening to a Conversation
Using Notes in a Presentation

Unit Theme

This unit is about the value of the past, with a focus on underwater discoveries including the wreck of the *Titanic* and lost parts of Cleopatra's world.

Unit 3 explores the topic of history as it relates to:
– underwater archaeology
– historical museums
– one city's historical district

– two famous shipwrecks
– early international trade

Think and Discuss *(page 41)*

5 mins

The coins and jewelry in the photo came from the *Whydah Galley*—an English trade ship. In 1717, it was captured by pirates in the Caribbean. Later that year, it sank in a storm off the coast of Massachusetts.

Much of the *Whydah's* gold and other treasures remained underwater until 1984, when the shipwreck was rediscovered by underwater explorer Barry Clifford.

This photo shows items with obvious monetary value, but the information that we gain from discoveries such as Clifford's is also very valuable.

▪ Discuss the questions.

▪ Give students information about the history of the *Whydah Galley*.

Pronunciation Note
Whydah: **whee**-dah

Exploring the Theme: Treasures from the Past *(pages 42-43)*

15 mins

The photos in the opening spread show divers exploring shipwrecks underwater.

TIP Exploit the photo on these pages by writing *wh-* question words on the board and then asking questions to stimulate discussion. For example:

T: <u>Who</u> do you see in this picture?
S: A diver. He or she is swimming.
T: Great! And <u>where</u> is this diver?

▪ Have students look at the photos and read the captions.

▪ Discuss the questions.

TIP You can discuss the Exploring the Theme questions as a whole class, or divide the class into pairs or small groups to discuss the questions.

Building and Using Vocabulary *(pages 44-45)*

30 mins

WARM-UP

- To introduce the topic of Cleopatra, have students look at the photos, map, and other information on these two pages.

- Ask a few questions to introduce the topic. For example:

  T: Who are we going to talk about?
  S: Cleopatra.
  T: Right, and who was Cleopatra?
  S: A queen?
  T: Yes, she was a queen. And where did Cleopatra live?
  S: Alexandria, Egypt.

Building Vocabulary

track 1-27

Exercise A. | Using a Dictionary

- Have students read the vocabulary words and check the words they already know.

- Play the audio so students can hear the vocabulary words.

- Give students time to look up any words they're not sure about in a dictionary.

Exercise B. | Have students match the words to their definitions.

> **Answer Key**   1. b 2. a 3. e 4. c 5. d

track 1-28

Exercise C. | Meaning from Context
Have students listen to the text as they read along in the Student Book.

> **Answer Key**   1. objects 2. image 3. exhibit 4. ruled 5. looked like

---

IDEAS FOR...   Checking Comprehension

To make sure students understood the short reading passage, ask a few questions using target vocabulary words. For example:

T: Did Cleopatra <u>rule</u> Egypt for a long time?
S: No, only for 20 years.
T: Did Cleopatra <u>rule</u> Egypt a long time ago?
S: Yes, she lived 2000 years ago.
T: Fifty years ago, did people know what Cleopatra <u>looked like</u>? When did we find out what she <u>looked like</u>?
S: No. We only found out recently.

Using Vocabulary

Exercise A. | Ask students to work individually to fill in the blanks with vocabulary words.

> **Answer Key**
>
> 1. nearby 2. ruled 3. image 4. looked like 5. recently 6. find 7. objects 8. dishes 9. tools

Exercise B. | Have students work in pairs to compare their answers for exercise **A**. Then have partners practice saying the conversations.

> **TIP**   Remind students to read each line and then look up to say the words to their partner. They should not be looking down at their books while they speak.

Exercise C. | Discussion   Have students discuss the questions in pairs. Make sure they recycle the target vocabulary as they personalize the topics of the unit thus far.

Pronunciation Note
Cleopatra: klee-uh-**pa**-truh

45 mins

Developing Listening Skills
(pages 46-47)

track 1-29
track 1-30

Pronunciation: The Simple Past Tense *-ed* Word Endings

Students learned about syllable number in Unit 1. The past tense *-ed* word endings affect syllable number, but only some of the time.

- Go over the information in the grammar box and then play the audio.

- Explain that the /t/ or /d/ endings sound very similar. (In the first set of examples, the sounds are /t/, /d/, and /d/.)

- In the second set of examples, the *-ed* ending adds an extra syllable to the word.

Answer Key

	/t/ or /d/	/əd/
1. painted		✓
2. explored	✓	
3. talked	✓	
4. divided		✓
5. closed	✓	
6. rested		✓
7. shouted		✓
8. watched	✓	

Before Listening

Understanding Visuals | Explain to students that the map of ancient Alexandria provides background knowledge for the upcoming listening passage.

Answer Key 1. T 2. T 3. F

Listening: A Talk about an Ancient City

In the first part of the listening passage, a museum guide welcomes visitors to an exhibit of objects from Cleopatra's world. Students hear about the real-life discoveries of explorer Franck Goddio.

track 1-31

Exercise A. | Listening for Main Ideas
Give students time to read over the incomplete sentences and answer choices before you play the audio.

Answer Key 1. b 2. a 3. b

Exercise B. | Note-Taking In the main listening passage, the tour guide gives additional information about Goddio's discoveries. The partially completed notes in this exercise are in the form of a T-chart, consisting of two headings and two columns of information. Have students practice listening for specific information. They will also see a model for the independent note-taking they are working toward.

track 1-32

Answer Key

1. 2000	5. containers	9. gods
2. 1984	6. tools	10. goddesses
3. ruins	7. ancient	
4. Underwater	8. palace (and temples)	

IDEAS FOR... **Expansion**

- Give students time to look up unfamiliar vocabulary from the listening passage (e.g., container, temple) in their dictionaries. Have them add these words to their vocabulary journals.
- Discuss syllable number of the words with *-ed* endings in exercise **B**. (*Started* is the only word with an added syllable.)

---

track 1-32

Exercise C. | Making Inferences

Answer Key 1. F 2. F 3. T

After Listening

Critical Thinking | Have pairs of students discuss the questions about the importance of museums.

Pronunciation Note
Antirhodos (Island): ahn-**tee**-row-dos
(Franck) Goddio: **gah**-dee-oh

Exploring Spoken English
(pages 48-50)

45 mins

Grammar: The Simple Past Tense

Go over the information in the grammar box. Keep in mind that most learners at this level have learned how to use the simple past tense to talk about the past, but the variables in the formation of the past tense form add a degree of difficulty.

Exercise A. | Have students work individually to complete the exercise.

Answer Key

2. lived **3.** moved, left **4.** tried **5.** read **6.** met

Exercise B. | Have students work in pairs to locate the words in the simple past tense. Then ask them to count the number of syllables in each past tense verb.

Answer Key

learned (1 syllable), took (1 syllable), heard (1 syllable), wanted (2 syllables), was (1 syllable), finished (2 syllables), Were (1 syllable), stopped (1 syllable), studied (2 syllables)

Exercise C. | Have partners practice the conversation in exercise **B**.

Language Function: Expressing Agreement Informally

In conversation, English speakers often use the expressions, *Me too* and *Me neither* to show that they agree with someone. This page provides information and practice so that students know which expression to use in any given situation.

> **TIP** If students are not familiar with the concept of affirmative versus negative statements, provide additional examples in two columns on the board.

Affirmative (yes)	Negative (no)
We saw Jason.	We didn't see Jason.
I speak Arabic.	I don't speak Arabic.
He can swim.	He can't swim.

Exercise A. | Have students complete the sentences on their own.

> **Answer Key**   **1.** too **2.** neither **3.** neither **4.** too

Exercise B. | Explain to students that Student A will read a statement from the left column, choosing the boldfaced verb that makes the sentence true for him or her. Student B will then agree or disagree using the target language *Me too* or *Me neither*. Afterward, Student B reads the statements from the right column and Student A agrees or disagrees with each statement.

Answer Key

Answers will vary with partners saying, "Me too" for affirmative statements and "Me neither" for negative statements.

Grammar: *Yes/No* Questions in the Simple Past Tense

> **TIP** If students found *yes/no* questions in the simple present tense difficult in Unit 1, review the grammar point before you go over the grammar box on page 50. (See the box below.)

> **IDEAS FOR...   Presenting Grammar**
>
> - Write two statements using the simple present tense on the board. For example:
>   1. Franck Goddio is very famous now.
>   2. The museum closes at 8:00 at night.
> - Call on students to ask a *yes/no* question about each statement. Edit the statements on the board so that they are correctly-formed *yes/no* questions. For example:
>   1. Is Franck Goddio very famous now?
>   2. Does the museum close at 8:00 at night?
> - Underline "is" in example 1, and "Does" and "close" in example 2.
> - Answer any questions students might have.

2. Did the *Titanic* arrive in New York in May? (No, it didn't. It never arrived in New York.)

3. Did all the passengers get into lifeboats? (No, they didn't.)

4. Did the *Titanic* sink at night? (Yes, it did.)

5. Did Ballard find the *Titanic* in the Atlantic Ocean? (Yes, he did.)

6. Did Ballard return in 1996? (No, he didn't. He returned in 1986.)

IDEAS FOR...   Expansion

Visit the *National Geographic* Web site to find articles, videos, photos, and audio programs about Bob Ballard's discoveries. Then direct your students to specific content you have found and give them a listening, reading, or writing assignment based on the content. You could also develop discussion questions to use in class, or use the Web site itself in class if you have computers with access to the Internet.

Speaking *(page 51)*

30-45 mins

Talking about the Past

Understanding Visuals | The time line shows the sequence of events in Bob Ballard's life—from a childhood interest in shipwrecks to his discovery of the *Titanic* and other underwater explorations.

- Direct students' attention to the photograph of Bob Ballard on page 50. Tell students they will read about events in Ballard's life.

- Give students time to read the time line. Encourage students to read page 215 of the *Independent Student Handbook* for more information on time lines.

- Conduct a brief class discussion of the time line so that students can ask any questions they might have.

Grammar: *Wh-* Questions in the Simple Past Tense

IDEAS FOR...   Presenting Grammar

- Use the time line to review the formation of *yes/no* questions in the simple past. Ask: *Did Ballard read books about shipwrecks as a child?*

- Go over the grammar box on page 51.

Discussion.

- Go over the directions. Ask for two student volunteers to read the speech bubbles aloud.

- Give another example of a wh- question:

    T: When did Ballard read about shipwrecks?
    S: He read about shipwrecks as a child.

- When you hear an error, repeat it with a questioning intonation. This lets students know that they should repeat the structure correctly.

- Write down a few of the correct examples that you hear. At the end of the activity, share the examples with the whole class.

IDEAS FOR...   Multi-level Classes

Planning pair or group tasks with students of mixed abilities can be a good way to involve everyone in the class and to create an atmosphere of teamwork. Make sure every student in the group has a specific job to do, and let the students work out for themselves which person does each job. For instance, you could change the discussion activity on page 51 and have Partner 1 find and point to content in the time line to ask a question about (e.g., "Ballard went to the area where the Titanic sank."). Have Partner 2 write down a question (e.g., Where did Ballard go on July 1, 1985?). Then have each pair join another pair to ask each other the questions they wrote.

Pronunciation Note
Titanic: tahy-**tan**-ik

Viewing: Treasures in Old San Juan *(pages 52-53)*

30 mins

Overview of the Video | San Juan, the capital of Puerto Rico, is one of the oldest European-founded cities in the Americas; only Santo Domingo in the Dominican Republic is older.

Old San Juan is the historical center of the city. In the video, residents remember problems that this part of San Juan had in the past, but also point out the vibrant culture and beautiful weather that attract people to Old San Juan today.

Before Viewing

Exercise A. | Have students activate their own knowledge of historical places and share the information with a partner.

Exercise B. | Identifying the Simple Past Tense Have students complete the exercise individually. Some of the video content is previewed while the simple past tense is reviewed.

Answer Key

came, became, were, protected

TIP Students may erroneously underline *called* in exercise B. Point out that this word is part of a reduced clause, "a fortress [that is] called . . . ," so it is not actually the simple past tense.

Exercise C. | Predicting Content

■ Go over the directions. Ask the class: *Can you predict anything about the video? What do we know about it?* The students might mention the title of the video, the photos on the pages, or the information from exercise **B** as clues for predicting what the video will be about.

Answer Key

Answers will vary, but most students will not check "an airport" or "new shopping centers" since the title of the video is "Old San Juan."

While Viewing

3:09 Exercise A. | Checking Predictions Have students watch the video for general understanding and to confirm the predictions they made in the previous exercise.

3:09 Exercise B. | Note-Taking After students watch the video again and take notes, give them a chance to share the things that interested them with the whole class, a partner, or a small group.

Answer Key *(Answers will vary.)*

3:09 Exercise C. | This exercise provides support to help students understand the speakers' statements.

Answer Key 1. b 2. c 3. a

After Viewing

Exercise A. | Discussion Have students discuss the questions in pairs. The focus of these questions is on summarizing information from the video and personalizing the topic.

Exercise B. | Using the Simple Past Tense This exercise provides additional information about the Spanish explorer Juan Ponce de Leon as well as practice with verbs in the simple past tense.

Answer Key 1. fought 2. became 3. gave 4. went 5. died

Building and Using Vocabulary (pages 54-55)

30 mins

Building Vocabulary

track 1-33

Exercise A. | Using a Dictionary

- Have students read the vocabulary words and check the ones they already know.

- Play the audio so students can hear the vocabulary words.

- Give students time to look up any words they're not sure about in a dictionary.

Exercise B. | Understanding Maps

The vocabulary and listening sections of Lesson B tell the true story of a shipwreck that happened in the ninth century. The map on this page shows the route the ship took from its home in the Middle East to its final resting place near Indonesia. Have students use the map to decide if the statements are true or false. If students have difficulty completing exercise **B**, have them revisit their answers here after completing exercise **C**.

Answer Key	1. T 2. T 3. F

Pronunciation Note
dhow: how

track 1-34

Exercise C. | Meaning from Context
Instruct students to choose the correct vocabulary word using the context of a short article about the shipwreck of the Arab *dhow*.

Answer Key

1. ship	5. silk
2. sailed	6. trade
3. everyday	7. Route
4. valuable	

Using Vocabulary

track 1-35

Exercise A.

- Give students time to read the article and fill in the blanks.

- Play the audio and let students listen and check their answers.

- Check to see that students understand verb tenses by doing items 1–3 as a class.

Answer Key

1. carry	5. everyday	9. route
2. sailed	6. silk	10. ship
3. traded	7. valuable	
4. goods	8. were made of	

Exercise B. | Discussion Encourage students to use target vocabulary words to discuss and expand on the topic.

TIP Depending on your goals and the size of your class, you can use these questions to conduct a whole-class discussion or a discussion for students to have in pairs or small groups.

Developing Listening Skills

45 mins

(pages 56-57)

Before Listening

Prior Knowledge

- Tell students that the listening section in this lesson has to do with the shipwreck they read about in the vocabulary section.
- Go over the directions and give partners time to remember or find the answers.

Answer Key *(Answers may vary.)*

1. It came from the Middle East.
2. It carried dishes, silk, and objects made of gold.
3. It sank between two islands/near Indonesia.
4. Divers found the *dhow*.

Listening: A Conversation

track 1-36

Exercise A. | Listening for Main Ideas

- Go over the directions. Give students time to read the questions and answer choices.
- Play the audio.

Answer Key   1. c 2. b 3. a

track 1-36

Exercise B. | Listening for Details

Repeat the procedure from exercise **A**.

Answer Key   1. a 2. a 3. c 4. b

After Listening

Exercise A. | Making Inferences   Asking students to make inferences gives them practice with a valuable critical thinking skill. It also encourages deeper processing of the language as they work with paraphrases rather than exact words as they explain the reasons for their choices.

- Go over the directions and give students time to decide if the statements are true or false.
- Ask partners to compare their answers and give reasons for them.

Answer Key   1. T 2. F 3. F

Exercise B. | Role-Playing

- Go over the information in the Student to Student box about making informal suggestions.
- Remind students of the homework assignment they heard about in the listening passage. (It was an individual assignment.)
- Ask students to imagine that they have to do a group homework assignment, and that each person in their group must write one paragraph on a specific topic.
- Go over the directions and the examples in the speech bubbles.
- When students have finished, have each group report on their topics to the whole class or to another group.

Exercise C. | Discussion   Have students discuss the questions with the same group members they worked with in exercise **C**.

> **TIP**   In exercise C, students have three distinct topics to discuss. Give them a time limit to talk about each question and keep track of the time while students are talking. For example:
>
> **T:**   OK, you have one minute to talk about question 1. . . Now you have two minutes to talk about question 2.

Exploring Spoken English
(pages 58-59)

30 mins

Grammar: Recognizing Past Tense Signal Words

IDEAS FOR... Presenting Grammar

- Write sentences on the board with time signal words and a choice of verb tenses.
  Ask students to choose the correct tense.
  For example:
  1. I (get / got) up at 7:00 every morning.
  2. I (buy / bought) a bus pass yesterday.
  3. The *Titanic* (sink / sank) in 1912.
  4. Joseph always (does / did) his homework on time.
  (Answers: **1.** get **2.** bought **3.** sank **4.** does)
- Ask students to tell you why they chose the simple present or simple past. If students are not sure of the reason, underline the signal words in the sentences.
- Go over the information in the grammar box on page 58.

Exercise A. | Have students use past tense signal words from the grammar box to fill in the blanks.

Answer Key	**2.** on **3.** Last **4.** In **5.** Last *Students should underline the following simple past tense verbs:* took, had, invented, went

Exercise B. | Have partners ask one another the questions and use their own ideas to answer.

Critical Thinking Focus: Recalling Facts

Exercise A. | Critical Thinking Talking about the past can lead us to the topic of remembering things from the past.

- Discuss the information in the Critical Thinking Focus box.
- Go over the directions for step 1 in the exercise and give students time to write their answers.
- Go over the directions for steps 2–4. Students listen to information from one partner and then say the information to a new partner.
- Ask students to talk about what they remembered and what they forgot.

track 1-37

Exercise B.

- Play the audio and have students read along in the Student Book.
- After students rank the ideas from 1 to 4, have them discuss their ideas with the class or with a partner.

Exercise C. | Collaboration Have groups of students work together to create a list of techniques for remembering information. They should then discuss the list in relation to language learning.

Engage: Using Notes in a Presentation *(page 60)*

45 mins

WARM-UP

- Before class, think of a few highlights from your own past that you want to share with the class.

- Write the highlights on the board in the form of a bulleted list. Begin each point with a verb in the simple past (e.g., "studied in New York").

- Tell the class that we can learn from each other's personal histories as well as from the histories of famous people such as Cleopatra.

- Give a brief presentation about yourself to model this Engage exercise using the notes on the board. Add a few interesting details and connect the ideas smoothly.

- End with a conclusion about why the events on the board were important to you.

Exercise A. | Planning a Presentation   In this activity, students prepare an individual presentation about their personal history using brief notes.

- Go over the directions. Give students time to think about past events in their lives that they want to tell the class about.

- Go over the information in the Presentation Skills box.

> **TIP**   Students may not want to talk about everything from their past lives. Encourage them to think about events they are comfortable sharing with the class.

Exercise B. | Organizing Ideas

- As a class, look at the sample presentation notes. Ask questions such as: *What will the student talk about first? Next? Why are the notes so short?*

- Give students time guidelines for their presentations, e.g., 2–3 minutes.

- Give students time to make notes for their own presentations. Remind them to write down only enough information to help them remember what they plan to talk about.

> **TIP**   If you have enough class time, give students a chance to practice their presentations. They can say their presentations quietly to themselves or to a partner.

Exercise C. | Presentation   Have students give their presentations to a group of classmates, or if the class is small enough, to the whole class.

Exercise D. | Self-Reflection   Encourage partners to reflect on their use of notes as well as how they felt during the individual presentations.

> **TIP**   Students appreciate feedback after a presentation, but it's often best to focus that feedback on the content or the target skill that was being practiced. In this case, give the class generalized feedback about how well they used their notes. For example:

T: Most of you used your notes very well. You wrote down only a little information, and you made eye contact with your audience. On the other hand, a few students tried to write down every word. Then they read sentences from their notes. That isn't the best way to give a presentation.

Pronunciation Note
Pusan: poo-**sahn**
Seoul: **sohl**

Weather and Climate

UNIT

4

Academic Track
Natural Science/
Environmental Science

Academic Pathways:
Lesson A: Listening to a Radio Show
            Planning an Itinerary
Lesson B: Listening to a Conversation
            among Friends
            Discussing Ways to Reduce
            Greenhouse Gases

Unit Theme

Unit 4 is about the weather—local conditions such as rain, wind, and high and low temperatures. It's also about the earth's climate—weather patterns over time.

Unit 4 examines the topics of weather and climate as they relate to:
– drought and flooding
– weather forecasting
– weather preferences
– climate change
– global rainfall trends

⏱ Think and Discuss *(page 61)*

5 mins

In one way or another, the earth's weather and climate affect every one of us. In places where the weather is quite variable, listening to a daily weather forecast helps people plan what they'll wear and what they'll do that day. Even in places where the weather doesn't change much from day to day, climate change is beginning to have a significant impact on nature and on the lives of the local people

- Discuss the questions.

- Give students some background information about the photo. Kansas City is in the central region of the United States, an area known as the Great Plains. Here, in this area of mostly flat, dry land, people usually welcome rain from a thunderstorm, but they're cautious of the dangers such as strong wind, lightning, and tornadoes.

⏱ Exploring the Theme: Weather and Climate *(pages 62-63)*

15 mins

The opening spread shows a thunderstorm in western Canada. Use the first question to review basic weather vocabulary and list the words on the board. For example:

T: What kinds of weather do you see on these pages?
S: I see lightning.
T: Good. In which picture?
S: In the big picture.
T: OK, and what other kinds of weather do you see?

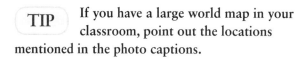
TIP If you have a large world map in your classroom, point out the locations mentioned in the photo captions.

- Point out the caption for each photo as you talk about it.

- Discuss the remaining questions about the photos.

- Have students read and answer the questions about the information in the chart.

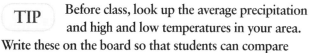
TIP Before class, look up the average precipitation and high and low temperatures in your area. Write these on the board so that students can compare them to the weather extremes in the chart.

Answer Key

Exercise B.

1. El Azizia, Libya (highest temperature)
Vostok, Antarctica (lowest temperature)

2. Lloro, Colombia (highest rainfall)
Arica, Chile (lowest rainfall)

Building and Using Vocabulary *(pages 64-65)*

30 mins

WARM-UP

- Point out the title of the article and the photographs.

- Ask students: *Which photo shows "too much water"? What's the word for this?* (The word "flooding" is in the photo caption.)

- Ask students: *Which photo shows "not enough water"? Do you know a word for this?* (Students may already know the word "drought." If not, tell them they will learn the word in this lesson.)

Building Vocabulary

track 1-38

Exercise A. | Using a Dictionary

- Have students read the vocabulary words and check the ones they already know.

- Play the audio so students can hear the vocabulary words.

- Give students time to look up any words they're not sure about in a dictionary.

Exercise B. | Meaning from Context

Give students time to read the article and choose the correct vocabulary words.

Answer Key

1. rainfall	5. drought	9. measure
2. amount	6. destroyed	10. forecasts
3. storms	7. temperature	
4. flooding	8. predict	

track 1-39

Exercise C. | Have students listen to the article from exercise **B** and check their answers.

IDEAS FOR... **Expansion**

The article in exercise **B** is a rich language source. Have students find three words in the article that they want to learn or want to remember. Ask them to share their list with a partner and explain their choices.

Using Vocabulary

Exercise A. | Have students complete the sentences by using the target vocabulary.

TIP Although there are only nine sentences in exercise A, there are ten blanks—one for each of the vocabulary words.

Answer Key

1. drought	4. amount	7. temperature
2. destroy	5. storm	8. measure
3. forecast	6. rainfall, flooding	9. predict

Exercise B. | Self-Reflection Have partners take turns asking and answering the questions using target vocabulary words to discuss their weather-related experiences and opinions.

IDEAS FOR... **Checking Comprehension**

After students discuss the questions in exercise **B**, call on one or two students at random to answer each question. Make this "reporting out" a bit more challenging by asking the questions in a random order—not the way they're arranged in the exercise. Pay attention to how well the students understand you and how well they answer in English.

Exercise C.

- Explain the exercise. On the left, there are five vocabulary words. On the right, there are five statements. Each statement is about one of the vocabulary words.

- Give students time to match the statements to the vocabulary words.

Answer Key   1. b 2. a 3. d 4. e 5. c

Developing Listening Skills

45 mins

(pages 66-67)

Before Listening

Exercise A. | Prior Knowledge Ask partners to discuss the ways people use weather forecasts. For example, the farmer might wait for dry, sunny weather to plant his crops. Depending on the forecast, the bride and groom might need to decide whether to get married indoors or outdoors. The people waiting for the bus certainly want to wear warm clothes for a cold, snowy day.

Exercise B. | Discussion Have each set of partners form a small group with another pair of students and discuss their answers from exercise **A**. Then have each group decide which people from the photos probably pay the most attention to weather forecasts.

Listening: A Radio Show

 track 1-40 **Exercise A. | Listening for Main Ideas**

- Give students time to read the questions and answer choices. Encourage students to read page 203 of the *Independent Student Handbook* for more information on listening for main ideas.

- Play the audio. Have students choose the correct answers.

   Answer Key 1. c 2. c 3. a

track 1-40 **Exercise B. | Listening for Details**

- Give students time to read the questions and answer choices.

- Play the audio a second time. Have students choose the correct answers.

   Answer Key 1. b 2. a 3. b 4. b 5. a

After Listening

Critical Thinking | Have students brainstorm possible reasons that weather forecasts are more accurate now than in the past. For example, they might say that satellites and other forms of technology give meteorologists better data to work with. Other factors might include better computers to work from and more sharing of information worldwide via the Internet. In addition to these high-tech factors, training for meteorologists could be improving as well.

Pronunciation: Reduced *of*

track 1-41

Reduced sounds in spoken English can add an extra challenge to listening comprehension. Learning some of the patterns of reduced speech can be quite helpful even if learners don't use the reductions in their own speech.

- Go over the information in the box.

- Play the audio so students can hear the examples.

- Have pairs of students practice saying reduced *of* in the six sentences.

TIP Tell students that learning about reduced sounds can improve their listening comprehension. For many language learners, however, using reduced sounds in their own speech may not be a good idea. Instead, their focus should be on pronouncing words as clearly as possible.

Exploring Spoken English
(pages 68-70)

45 mins

Language Function: Expressing Likes and Dislikes

track 1-42
Exercise A.

- Go over the information in the box. Remind students that in a conversation, we often want to share our opinions, for example, when we talk about things we like and dislike.

- Play the audio as students read along in the Student Book.

Exercise B. | Have students practice the interview in pairs and identify four different ways the speakers express likes and dislikes.

Answer Key

Students should underline the following expressions:
I really like it.
I hate it . . .
I loved it!
I can't stand it!

Exercise C. | Encourage students to make several statements using the expressions and topics from the box.

TIP Since the sentences in exercise C are brief, turn the activity into fluency practice by having students repeat the exercise once or twice with new partners. This gives them a chance to say and hear some of the sentences more than once.

Exercise D. | Discussion

- Divide the class into small groups.

- Go over the directions. Each group member gives an opinion about each topic.

- Have students generate two or more new topics of conversation.

IDEAS FOR...   Multi-level Classes

At the end of exercise **D**, calling on students to share their opinions with the class is a good way to give everyone a chance to participate and feel successful. Since students have already practiced the expressions, they should feel quite prepared to answer you. For example:

T: Lorena, how do you feel about science classes?
S: I love them!
T: Good for you! And Jin, how do you feel about sports?
S: I dislike sports.
T: I understand. I don't like sports either.

Grammar: Count and Noncount Nouns

IDEAS FOR...   Presenting Grammar

- Make simple line drawings of three flowers on the board.

- Ask students: *How many flowers do you see?* (three)

- Now draw many small lines to represent rain. Tell students: *It's raining. How many rain? One, two, three?* Encourage students to correct you by saying: *How **much** rain?*

- Explain that in many languages, there are some things we can count, such as flowers, and some things we cannot count, such as rain.

- Go over the information in the box.

Exercise A. | Using a Dictionary

Have students work in pairs to complete the chart. Note that the answers to this exercise may vary due to the literary usage of the word (i.e., the *waters* of the Nile, the *sands* of time). These answers represent common usage.

Answer Key

Count	Noncount	Both Count and Noncount
street	water	drought
cloud	snow	food
person	flooding	
	thunder	
	wind	
	lightning	
	sand	

TIP To reinforce the most common count and noncount usages of the nouns in exercise A, use the words in sentences as you go over the answers. For example:

T: What kind of noun is *water*?

S: It's a noncount noun.

T: Right. *There is a little water in the glass.* And what kind of noun is "street"?

S: It's a count noun.

T: Good. *There are two very busy streets in this city.*

Exercise B. |
Have partners practice using count and noncount nouns in a free conversation about the photo. Some of the topics they choose to talk about may include the following: *wind, water, people, trees, houses,* and *things to do.*

Exercise C.

- Go over the information in the chart.

- Have students fill in the blanks with expressions from the chart.

Answer Key

1. inch of	**3.** inches of	**5.** sheets of
2. gust of	**4.** clap of	**6.** piece of

Speaking *(page 71)*

30-45 mins

Planning an Itinerary

In this activity, groups of students plan a vacation itinerary using a weather forecast to help them plan their daily activities.

- Go over the information in the Critical Thinking Focus box.

- **Step 1:** Students discuss which vacation activities they enjoy and add their own ideas to the list.

- **Step 2:** Students read the weather forecast for their vacation weekend.

- **Step 3:** Using the information in the weather forecast, students choose two appropriate activities for each day of their vacation.

> **IDEAS FOR...   Expansion**
>
> To expand on the itinerary activity and review the simple past tense, have students write journal entries for one or more days of the vacation they planned. They should use their imagination to write about where they went, what they did, and how the weather was. Follow up by reading the journal entries yourself and making written comments on them, or by having students read and comment on each other's work.

Viewing: Tornado Chase

30 mins

(pages 72-73)

WARM-UP

Overview of the Video | When dangerous storms such as tornadoes are nearby, most people want to escape the danger—but not Tim Samaras. For this severe-storms researcher, a tornado is an opportunity to gain valuable data. The data help scientists to understand how tornadoes form and move, and the information helps them to predict where tornadoes will occur in the future. As you'll see in this video clip, Samaras's research puts him in some very thrilling situations.

Before Viewing

Use the video's title and the photos on these pages to prepare students for the video.

- Point to the title and photo on page 72. Ask: *What is this video about?* (tornadoes) *What do you know about tornadoes?*

- Point to the photos on page 73. Ask: *What questions do you have about the photos?*

- Listen to students' comments and questions with interest. Tell students they will find out more when they watch the video.

Exercise A. | Critical Thinking Have partners collaborate to create a list of ways weather can be dangerous. Then have them discuss dangerous weather in their country.

Exercise B. | Using a Dictionary Important vocabulary and background information are presented in the context of facts about tornadoes.

Exercise C. | Have students discuss the questions in pairs.

While Viewing

Exercise A.
3:57

- Go over the directions.

- Give students time to read the answer choices.

- Play the video with or without the captions. Have students choose the correct answers.

> **Answer Key**
>
> find a road that takes them close to the tornado
>
> deploy all of Tim Samaras's probes
>
> escape from a tornado

Exercise B.
3:57

- Give students time to read the sentences and the answer choices.

- Play the video a second time. For a more challenging task, turn the captions off.

Answer Key   1. b 2. c 3. a 4. b

After Viewing

Critical Thinking | Have students work in small groups to discuss the questions and perform critical thinking tasks such as speculating, relating information to one's own life, evaluating, and forming judgments.

> **IDEAS FOR...   Expansion**
>
> In the video, the narrator explained that the tornado was an F-4 tornado. Explain that F-4 is a ranking on the Fujita Scale—a scale that scientists use to rank the intensity of a tornado. Ask students to research the Fujita Scale on the Internet and take brief notes on the different rankings. Then discuss the scale as a class. Encourage students to share information they learned from their research.

Building and Using Vocabulary *(pages 74-75)*

30 mins

WARM-UP

Write the words *weather* and *climate* on the board. Point to each word and ask: *What does this word mean?* Students should know the meaning of *weather* from Lesson A. They may not know how to define *climate*, but the reading in exercise **A** begins with a definition of that word.

Building Vocabulary

track 1-43

Exercise A. | Meaning from Context

The Lesson B vocabulary is presented in the context of a short article about climate change.

- Play the audio and have students read along in the Student Book.

- Give students time to read the article again at their own pace.

Exercise B. | Have students use context clues in the article to write each vocabulary word next to its definition.

Answer Key

1. coast	**5.** rise	**9.** instead of
2. melting	**6.** patterns	**10.** exist
3. average	**7.** heat	
4. somewhat	**8.** grow	

Using Vocabulary

Exercise A. | Have students work in pairs to complete the sentences that contain some of the target vocabulary.

Answer Key *(Answers will vary.)*

Exercise B. | This exercise provides background information for the listening section of Lesson B. Students use all except one of the terms in the box to fill in the blanks.

Answer Key

1. rising **2.** pattern **3.** instead of **4.** melting **5.** heat (The word "coast" is not used.)

Exercise C. | Critical Thinking Have students discuss the questions in small groups.

IDEAS FOR... Checking Comprehension

To do a quick check of students' vocabulary comprehension, prepare an oral or written quiz with 10 questions that contain the target words. Be sure to use grammar structures that the students are familiar with. Ask questions such as the following:

1. What kinds of fruit <u>grow</u> in our part of the world?
2. Does the sun <u>rise</u> in the morning or in the evening?
3. What school subject is <u>somewhat</u> difficult for you? What subject is very difficult?
4. Besides ice, what are some other things that can <u>melt</u>?
5. Tell me one thing that did not <u>exist</u> before 1990.

Developing Listening Skills

45 mins

(pages 76-77)

Before Listening

Activating Prior Knowledge | The information in this box stresses the importance of activating prior knowledge. Language learners can improve their listening comprehension by asking themselves what they already know about the topic.

Exercise A. | Critical Thinking Have students make a list of things they already know about the effects of climate change on Greenland.

Exercise B. | Have partners compare their lists from exercise **A** and discuss which items on their lists they're likely to hear about.

Listening: A Conversation among Friends

 track 1-44

Exercise A. | Listening for Context

- Give students time to read the questions.

- Play the audio. Have students write answers to the questions.

Answer Key

1. They are friends.

2. He lives in Greenland.

3. They live in Canada.

4. They are eating dinner together and talking.

 track 1-44

Exercise B. | Note-Taking Play the audio again. Have students listen and complete the notes in the T-chart.

Answer Key *(Student notes may vary.)*

Benefits (good things)	Drawbacks (bad things)
1. Growing more trees, foods, grass	1. Possible for oil to get into ocean water
2. People may get oil	2. Rising sea levels (bad for cities on coast)

 track 1-44

Exercise C. | Listening for Details

- Give students time to read the questions and answer choices.

- Play the audio again. Have students choose the correct answers.

Answer Key   1. a 2. a 3. c

After Listening

Exercise A. | Self-Reflection Have students discuss the questions in pairs. Explain that the focus of these questions is to personalize the issues raised in the listening passage.

Exercise B. | Role-Playing Go over the information in the Student to Student box. In groups of three, have students continue the conversation from the listening passage.

TIP To help students get comfortable with the idea of role-playing, model it for them first. When a role-play only involves two speakers, you can model a conversation yourself using two different "voices." You can even stand in a different position for each speaker. In this case, since the role-play involves three speakers, call on two of your higher-level students to help you. Then the three of you can stand at the front of the class and demonstrate the role-play activity. Try to create an atmosphere of low-stress fun.

Exploring Spoken English
(pages 78-79)

30 mins

Grammar: *A, An, Any,* and *Some*

IDEAS FOR... **Presenting Grammar**

- Go over the information and examples in the box.

- If students aren't sure when to use *a* or *an*, write several countable nouns on the board. As you say each word, emphasize its initial sound and ask: A or an? Write the correct article before each word and explain that *a* is used with words beginning with a consonant sound, and *an* is used with words beginning with a vowel sound.

- Alternatively, you can present the information from the box in a different way:
  1. Explain that *a* or *an* means *one* so the words are used with singular nouns in statements and questions.
  2. *Some* is used with plural or noncount nouns in statements and questions.
  3. *Any* is also used with plural or noncount nouns, but usually only in negative statements and in questions.

Exercise A. | Have students work individually to fill in the blanks in the conversation with *a*, *an*, *any*, and *some*.

Answer Key   1. a 2. any 3. Some 4. some 5. a

Exercise B. | Have students compare their answers from exercise **A** with a partner and then practice the conversation.

Exercise C. | Using *a, an, any,* and *some*
Have students read the questions and underline *a*, *an*, *any*, and *some* individually before they discuss them in pairs.

Language Function: Comparing Quantities or Amounts

Go over the information in the box with students. Answer any questions they may have.

Exercise A. | Understanding Visuals
Have students work in groups of three or four to interpret the map and discuss projected future rainfall patterns in different regions. Encourage students to read page 216 of the *Independent Student Handbook* for more information on interpreting and understanding visuals.

Answer Key *(Answers will vary.)*

1. Areas such as Greenland, northeastern Africa, and central Asia will get a lot more rain. Areas such as southern South America and northern Africa will get a lot less rain.

2. Areas such as northern Asia will get a little more rain. Areas such as central South America will get a little less rain.

TIP   Students can stay in their small groups for both exercise A and exercise B if you prefer instead of getting into pairs.

Exercise B. | Collaboration   Have students work together to create a list of countries that will likely get more or less rain in future years.

Answer Key *(Answers will vary.)*

Countries such as Canada, Greenland, Egypt, and Norway will get more rain. Countries such as Mexico, Spain, Sudan, and most of Australia will get less rain.

TIP   Since only a few countries are labeled on the rainfall map, students can use their prior knowledge or a world map to locate more countries.

45
mins

Engage: Discussing Ways to Reduce Greenhouse Gases
(page 80)

WARM-UP

In the Lesson B vocabulary and listening sections, students learned about some of the effects of climate change. This activity focuses on global warming—one kind of climate change.

- Write *climate change* and *global warming* on the board and ask students what each term means.

- Remind students of the warming that is happening in Greenland. Ask them to name some benefits and drawbacks of warmer temperatures from page 77.

Exercise A. | Note-Taking
track 1-45

- Go over the directions. Have students take notes on the effects of greenhouse gases on global warming.

- Play the audio. Have students listen and take brief notes.

Exercise B. | Understanding Visuals
Have students use the chart, their notes, and their prior knowledge to discuss the process of global warming—both its causes and its effects.

Exercise C. | Collaboration   Have students work
in pairs to rank the ways greenhouse gases can be reduced.

TIP   As you monitor students' discussions, encourage them to consider how each item in the list reduces greenhouse gases. For example, using less electricity at home might mean fewer power plants will be built. On the other hand, some kinds of power plants (e.g., geothermal or hydroelectric) don't produce a lot of greenhouse gases, so using less electricity might not be the most helpful way to reduce greenhouse gases.

Presentation Skills: Making Eye Contact |
Go over the information in the box. Model the difference between an adequate amount of eye contact and not enough eye contact.

Exercise D. | In small groups, have students practice making eye contact while speaking as they compare their rankings from exercise **C** and explain the reasons for them.

> **IDEAS FOR...   Expansion**
>
> Use the term *global warming* in an Internet search engine to find Web sites and videos related to the topic. (Try to locate a video where the language used is appropriate for language learners.) Choose one of the Web sites or videos that you find and create a homework assignment based on it.

Focus on Food

Academic Track
Interdisciplinary

Academic Pathways:
Lesson A: Listening to a Talk by an
Anthropology Professor
Conducting a Survey

Lesson B: Listening to a Conversation
between Students
Creating a Description with
Interesting Details

Unit Theme

Unit 5 focuses on food—especially on the foods that we love, and the foods that make us say, "Ugh, that's disgusting!"

Unit 5 explores the topic of food as it relates to:

– unusual foods
– food and travel
– opinions about food

– staple foods
– restaurants and cafeterias
– descriptions of food

 # Think and Discuss: *(page 81)*

5 mins

Everyone has opinions about food. Food is not only necessary for staying alive, but it is also closely attached to our culture and our experiences with home and family.

- Point out the unit title and the Academic Pathways at the top of the page. These items will give students a preview of the unit.

- Discuss the questions.

- Encourage students to comment on the photo. For example:

T: What are these people doing?
S: They're drying apricots.
T: That's right. Do you like to eat apricots?

 # Exploring the Theme: Focus on Food *(pages 82-83)*

15 mins

The opening spread features a photograph of a large banana plantation in Rwanda, where a river provides the large amounts of water needed to grow this fruit. As is the case everywhere, the food that farmers can grow depends on climate and geographical conditions.

- Have students look at the photos and read the captions.

- Discuss the questions.

- Encourage students to ask questions and express their opinions as you go through the discussion questions.

TIP Some of the foods pictured in the opening spread may be unfamiliar to students, or they may have strong feelings about them. Encourage students to share their opinions about each food pictured.

Building and Using Vocabulary *(pages 84-85)*

30 mins

WARM-UP

- Ask the class about a few foods you think most of them will like. For example: *How many of you like apples?*

- Then ask about some foods you think students will not like, or that they will find strange. For example: *How many of you like frog legs? How about old cheese? Do you like that?*

- Tell students they will learn about some interesting kinds of food in this lesson.

Building Vocabulary

track 2-2

Exercise A. | Meaning from Context

- Direct students' attention to the photos and captions at the top of page 84.

- Play the audio and have students read the sentences in the Student Book.

Exercise B. | Encourage students to use context clues from the sentences in exercise **A** to match the words to the definitions.

Answer Key

1. allow	**5.** only	**9.** nutritious
2. raw	**6.** delicious	**10.** taste
3. touch	**7.** local	
4. unusual	**8.** imagine	

Using Vocabulary

Exercise A.

- Give students time to read through the article and fill in the blanks.

- Discuss the content of the article.

TIP Ask students to do exercise A without using a dictionary since they already have definitions for the words on page 84. If there are other words from the article students want to look up afterwards, let them use a dictionary at that time.

Answer Key

1. local	**5.** taste	**9.** allow
2. only	**6.** touch	**10.** nutritious
3. imagine	**7.** raw	
4. delicious	**8.** unusual	

IDEAS FOR... **Checking Comprehension**

To make sure students have understood the main ideas from the article on page 85, write the following question words on the board: *Who? What? Where? How? Why?*

Lead a class discussion, asking students:
Who is the article about?
What is Dr. Davis's job?
Where does the durian fruit grow?
How do people eat durian fruit?
Why does Dr. Davis eat unusual foods?

Exercise B. | Self-Reflection Have students complete the sentences with their own ideas and then share them with a partner.

Developing Listening Skills

45 mins

(pages 86-87)

Before Listening

Prior Knowledge | In the Lesson A listening passage, a professor delivers a talk and answers questions from her students. This activity gives students a chance to reflect on their own experiences of asking questions in class. Remind students that there are no right answers to the questions in this exercise, and keep in mind that students' ideas about this topic will vary by culture, age, and other factors.

Listening: A Talk by an Anthropology Professor

Exercise A. | Listening for Main Ideas

track 2-3

- Give students time to read the questions and answer choices.

- Play the audio. Have students choose the correct answers.

    Answer Key   1. c 2. a 3. c

Exercise B.

track 2-3

- Give students time to review the list in the Before Listening section.

- Play the audio again. Have students listen for how questions are asked in the listening passage.

    Answer Key

    ✓ Raise your hand and say the professor's name.

    ✓ Use a phrase such as *Could I ask a question?* or *I have a question.*

    ✓ Just ask your question when there is a quiet moment.

Exercise C. | Listening for Details

track 2-3

- Give students time to read the sentences.

- Play the audio again. Have students complete the sentences with the words they hear.

Answer Key

1. community 2. honey 3. (starchy) vegetable
4. sick 5. travels 6. cheese

After Listening

Exercise A. | Self-Reflection   Have students reflect on their own eating habits in small groups.

Exercise B. | Critical Thinking   Have students discuss the questions in groups of three or four as they focus on the relationship between culture and food.

IDEAS FOR...   **Expansion**

For homework, challenge your students to try one new food that they have never eaten before. (You may want to point out that this food doesn't have to be very unusual; it should simply be a food they have never eaten.) Give students a week to try this food and have them report on the experience afterwards. Ask them to describe finding and preparing the new food, tasting it for the first time, and whether or not they have plans to eat it again. Have students give short presentations to the whole class or to a small group.

Pronunciation: *Can and Can't*

track 2-4

It's difficult for learners to distinguish between *can* and *can't* in spoken English, so it's helpful to know that the /t/ sound is not the only difference in the way the two words are pronounced: *Can't* is pronounced with the full vowel sound /æ/, while *can* usually has the reduced schwa sound /ə/.

- Go over the information in the box.

- Play the audio.

- Have students practice saying the sentences in exercise **A** in pairs.

Exploring Spoken English

(pages 88-90)

track 2-5

Language Function: Expressing Opinions

Like many language functions, expressing opinions has a social component. The expressions we use to show that a statement is an opinion are also a way to soften or hedge the statement so that we don't sound overly forceful or adamant. Play the audio and have students read along in the Student Book.

Exercise A. | Have students underline expressions from the Language Function box in the conversations.
track 2-6

Answer Key

1. **Lydia:** <u>I think</u> these fried potatoes are delicious.

   Henri: <u>I don't think</u> they're good for you, though.

   Lydia: You're probably right.

   Henri: <u>Personally</u>, I don't like to eat any fried foods.

2. **Lee:** Do you like the chicken curry?

   Zachary: <u>In my opinion</u>, it's a little too hot.

   Lee: Really? <u>For me</u>, it's perfect.

3. **Natalia:** What are you cooking? It smells great!

   Jenny: It's *falafel*. It's a vegetarian dish.

   Natalia: Are you making any meat dishes to go with it?

   Jenny: Not tonight. <u>Personally</u>, <u>I think</u> we eat too much meat.

Exercise B. | Have students practice the conversations from exercise **A** in pairs.

Exercise C. | Have students work in pairs to complete the statements with expressions from the box and then practice saying the statements.

TIP The expressions for giving opinions vary in their grammar and meaning, so not every expression can be used in every case. Monitor your students as they practice and help them to choose appropriate expressions.

Answer Key *(Answers will vary.)*

1. **A:** <u>If you ask me</u>, puffer fish is too dangerous for people to eat.

   B: <u>I think</u> you're right.

2. **A:** <u>In my opinion</u>, eating insects is a terrible idea.

   B: <u>Personally</u>, I would like to try them.

3. **A:** <u>I think</u> Frank is a very good chef.

   B: <u>I don't think</u> he cooks eggs very well, however.

Grammar: *Can* and *Can't*

IDEAS FOR...   Presenting Grammar

Go over the information in the grammar box.
To help students grasp the different uses of *can* and *can't*, provide additional examples as you go over the chart. For example:

T: What are some of your abilities? Lisa, <u>can</u> you sing?

S: Yes, I <u>can</u>.

T: That's great! I <u>can't</u> sing very well, but I like to hear people who <u>can</u> sing.

Exercise A. | Have students work individually to complete the sentences.

Answer Key 1. can't 2. can 3. can't
4. can 5. can 6. can't

Exercise B. | In this activity, students practice grammar as well as pronunciation. Have them ask each other questions using the reduced pronunciation of *can* and give short answers containing full vowel sounds.

Exercise C.

- Play the audio and have students read along in the Student Book.

- Have students go through the article and underline the uses of *can* and *can't*.

> **TIP** In exercise C, you can place more focus on listening by asking students to close their books. Then play the audio and check students' comprehension before doing the rest of the activity.

Answer Key

. . . chocolate <u>can</u> have up to 60 insect parts, and peanut butter <u>can</u> have 30 insect fragments . . .

Tomato sauce <u>can't</u> contain more than 30 fly eggs per 3.5 ounces (100 grams).

And food is not the only place you <u>can</u> find insects and insect parts.

The fact is—you <u>can't</u> always avoid eating insects.

Exercise D. | Have students use the article in exercise **C** to answer the questions.

Answer Key

1. No, it can't. 2. No, you can't. 3. Yes, they can.
4. No, it can't. 5. Yes, it can. 6. No, they can't.

Exercise E. | **Critical Thinking** As students discuss the questions in groups of three or four, encourage them to go beyond the information in the article to form reasoned opinions.

Speaking *(page 91)*

30-45 mins

Conducting a Survey

Oftentimes, the foods that are linked most closely to a culture are its staple foods. Whether they're corn and beans in Mexico, rice in Vietnam, or wheat pasta in Italy, a region's staple foods are eaten by many of its people every day. They are known as the "common denominator" of its cuisine, and represent a cultural bond that ties people together.

Exercise A. | **Note-Taking** Have students use the chart to interview three of their classmates.

> **TIP** Have students stand up and walk around the classroom as they conduct their surveys. This will liven up the activity and alter the usual classroom routine.

Exercise B. | **Critical Thinking** Have students consider the information they gathered in their surveys and decide which information is worth talking about.

> **TIP** In exercise B, students plan the presentation they will give in exercise C. Go over the directions for exercise C in advance so that students know what to expect.

Exercise C. | **Presentation** In small groups, have students report on their surveys.

IDEAS FOR... **Multi-level Classes**

Divide the class into groups for exercise **C** in a way that mixes higher-level and lower-level students. This way, lower-level students benefit from hearing presentations given by higher-level students, who in turn benefit from supporting their lower-level classmates.

Viewing: Forbidden Fruit
(pages 92-93)

30 mins

Overview of the Video | It is said that some foods are "an acquired taste," which means that with enough time and exposure, we can learn to love them. One of these foods is a kind of fruit from southeastern Asia. It's called durian fruit, and it looks and tastes unusual. But for hotel owners in this video clip, it's not the durian's appearance or taste that's a problem—it's the durian's strong smell. (Refer students back to the reading on page 85 for more information on durian fruit.)

TIP Since durian fruit isn't found everywhere, students may be curious about it. Some Asian markets sell packages of frozen durian fruit at a reasonable price, and you may consider bringing some to class for students to try.

Before Viewing

Exercise A. | Critical Thinking As students discuss the questions in pairs, tell them to try to recall information from Lesson A as they analyze reasons for disliking certain foods.

Exercise B. | Using a Dictionary Have students use a dictionary to complete the T-chart.

Answer Key

Positive Meaning	Negative Meaning
fragrant	awful
precious	disgusting
	smelly
	smuggle

While Viewing

Exercise A.
2:29

- Give students time to read the sentences.

- Play the video without the captions. Have students watch the video and choose the correct answers.

Answer Key   1. c 2. b 3. b 4. c

Exercise B.
2:29

- Play the video again without the captions.

- Have students listen and look at the list of words from the Before Viewing section.

After Viewing

track 2-8

Exercise A. | Meaning from Context Play the audio and have students read along in the Student Book.

TIP Alternatively, give students time to read the text at their own pace. Then play the audio and have students read along.

Exercise B. | Have students work in pairs to complete the exercise.

Answer Key   1. vigil 2. war 3. front lines 4. alert

Exercise C. | Expressing Opinions In small groups, have students discuss the questions.

TIP Remind students to use expressions from the box on page 88 for giving opinions.

Building and Using Vocabulary *(pages 94-95)*

30 mins

WARM-UP

The Lesson B vocabulary is presented in the context of an article about three types of restaurants.

- Help students preview the article by pointing out the title, the three headings, and the photos. Ask: *What kinds of restaurants are you going to learn about?*

Building Vocabulary

track 2-9

Exercise A. | Meaning from Context

- Ask students where they usually eat. *Do you eat at home? At a school cafeteria? At a restaurant?*

- Write the names of some restaurants your students know about on the board. Ask them why they like each one.

- Tell students they will learn about three interesting kinds of restaurants in this section.

- Play the audio as students read along in the Student Book.

Using Vocabulary

Exercise A. | Have students complete the sentences using the target vocabulary words.

Answer Key

1. order	5. serve	9. numerous
2. liquid	6. quickly	10. treats
3. neighborhood	7. meet	
4. popular	8. beverage	

> **IDEAS FOR...** **Checking Comprehension**
>
> At this point, students have encountered the vocabulary words in two different contexts, but they have not used their dictionaries. For variety and communicative practice, ask the class if they're unsure about any of the vocabulary words. Then give brief verbal explanations and other example sentences as you discuss the words.

Exercise B. | Collaboration Have students work in pairs to categorize each vocabulary word according to its grammatical function in exercise **A**.

Answer Key

Noun	Verb
liquid	order
neighborhood	serve
beverage	meet
treat	

Adjective	Adverb
popular	quickly
numerous	

Exercise C. | Have students ask and answer the questions in pairs.

Developing Listening Skills
(pages 96-97)

45 mins

Before Listening

track 2-10
Listening for Specific Information

- Go over the information in the box.

- Play the audio and have students read along in the Student Book.

- Point out the information the listener needed as well as the information that wasn't needed.

track 2-11
Note-Taking

- Give students time to read the questions.

- Play the audio. Have students take notes to answer the questions.

Answer Key *(Answers may vary.)*

1. on the first floor of South Hall

2. anyone can eat there (open to the public)

3. from 6:30 a.m until 7:00 p.m.

4. $3.50 for breakfast; $5.00 for dinner (more if you're not a student)

Listening: A Conversation between Students

track 2-12
Exercise A. | Listening for Main Ideas

- Go over the directions and give students time to read the questions and answer choices.

- Play the audio. Have students choose the correct answers.

Answer Key   1. a 2. b 3. b

track 2-12
Exercise B. | Listening for Details

- Give students time to read the statements.

- Play the audio a second time. Have students decide if the statements are true or false. Ask them to make the necessary changes to turn the false statements into true statements.

Answer Key

1. F (Roger thinks the cafeteria coffee is bad.) 2. F (Roger usually eats dinner around 8:00 or 9:00.) 3. T 4. T 5. T

After Listening

Exercise A. | Self-Reflection   Have students rank the items according to their own ideas about eating at restaurants.

Exercise B.

- Go over the information in the Student to Student box.

- Have partners discuss their rankings from exercise **A** while they practice showing agreement.

> **TIP** The speech bubbles on this page illustrate a kind of agreement that isn't shown in the box. Point out that the phrase "me too" in the second speech bubble is another way to agree with someone else's ideas or statements.

Exercise C. | Critical Thinking   Have students discuss the questions in groups of four.

30 mins

Exploring Spoken English
(pages 98-99)

Exercise A. | Have students listen to the conversation as they read along in the Student Book.

IDEAS FOR... **Presenting Grammar**

For some learners, an inductive approach to grammar works best. In this case, the conversation contains the target grammar—descriptive adjectives. Students have an opportunity to see adjectives used in a context and work out some of the usage patterns for themselves.

- Play the audio and have students read along in the Student Book.
- Ask students to tell you some of the words for describing food that they noticed such as *delicious, fresh, warm, little,* and *raw.*
- Tell students that these words are all adjectives. Then ask a few questions to raise students' awareness of how adjectives are used. For example:

  T: Delicious. According to these students, what foods are delicious?

  S1: Tacos! Tacos are delicious.

  T: And tortillas . . . what kind of tortillas do they talk about?

  S2: Fresh tortillas!

  T: So tacos are delicious. We eat fresh tortillas. . . . So, where can we use adjectives in a sentence?

Exercise B. | Have students practice the conversation from exercise **A** in pairs.

Grammar: Descriptive Adjectives

Exercise A. | Go over the information in the box. Give students time to write sentences on their own. Have students read their sentences to a partner.

Answer Key *(Answers will vary.)*

2. The soup at the Blue Moon Café is salty.

3. I really like fried eggs.

4. My favorite snack is crunchy potato chips.

5. This apple tastes sweet.

6. I don't like spicy foods.

TIP As students share their sentences in exercise A, encourage them to monitor their own grammatical accuracy as well as their partner's. Encourage them to ask you any questions they might have.

Exercise B. | Describing a Favorite Food
Have students think about a favorite food and how they will describe the food to a partner.

Exercise C. | Have students use descriptive adjectives as they describe the food they chose in exercise **B**.

Critical Thinking Focus: Distinguishing between Main Ideas and Details | The information in this Critical Thinking Focus box helps to prepare students for the Engage page that follows, which has students create descriptions using adjectives and interesting details. Have students complete the exercise in pairs.

Answer Key

Left box:	Right box:
1. D 2. D 3. D 4. M	1 . D 2. M 3. D 4. D

Engage: Creating a Description with Interesting Details

(page 100)

45 mins

In this exercise, students work in groups of three to create tempting descriptions of food for a restaurant menu. Go over the information in the Situation box.

- Point out the three menu items in the photos.

- Divide the class into groups of three.

> **TIP** This activity can be teacher-led, with the teacher doing things such as reading the directions aloud and keeping track of the time. It can also be student-led. Ask for a volunteer from each group to manage the activity.

Step 1: Discussion | Have students work together to generate details about the three menu items in the photos.

Step 2: Brainstorming | Have students brainstorm a list of descriptive adjectives to describe the three menu items.

Step 3: Planning a Presentation | Instruct each group member to work on a description of one of the menu items.

> **TIP** If a group has four students instead of three, ask two students to work together to describe one menu item.

Presentation Skills: Giving Interesting Details | Go over the information in the Presentation Skills box. Give students an example sentence and ask them to provide additional details to make the sentence more interesting.

Step 4: Presentation

- Encourage students to read pages 211-213 of the *Independent Student Handbook* for some more information about classroom presentation skills.

- Have students present their descriptions to their group. Tell group members to provide feedback and suggestions for improvement.

IDEAS FOR... Expansion

Many restaurants offer paper menus for customers to take home with them. To reinforce the idea of using descriptive adjectives and interesting details, either gather some of these menus yourself or ask students to find them and bring them to class. Have students locate adjectives in the menu descriptions and evaluate the menus in pairs or small groups.

Housing

Academic Track
Interdisciplinary

Academic Pathways:
Lesson A: Listening to a PowerPoint Presentation
            Expressing Relationships between Ideas
Lesson B: Listening to a Conversation
            Role-Playing a Meeting with
            Real Estate Agents

Unit Theme

Unit 6 is about the buildings we call home—apartments, condominiums, and houses. The unit discusses practical and aesthetic considerations as well as environmental concerns associated with housing.

Unit 6 looks at the topic of housing as it relates to:

– architect Antoni Gaudí
– real estate agents and clients
– housing options

– *trompe l'oeil* painting
– housing development
– straw houses

Think and Discuss *(page 101)*

5 mins

The human need for shelter makes the topic of housing something we all have in common. On the other hand, the incredible variety of homes in which we live makes the topic quite interesting.

■ Point out the unit title and the Academic Pathways at the top of the page. These items will give students a preview of the unit.

■ Discuss the questions. Encourage students to comment on the house in the photograph.

Exploring the Theme: Housing *(pages 102-103)*

15 mins

As the earth's population continues to grow, so does the need for more housing. The large photo in the opening spread is of a housing development in Dubai, United Arab Emirates. Here, the demand for waterfront property combined with great wealth has given rise to the artificial islands of the Palm Jumeirah development in the Persian Gulf. A highway and a monorail train transport residents from the mainland to the costly houses.

■ Have students look at the photos and read the captions.

■ Discuss the questions.

> **TIP** Students may or may not have the world knowledge needed to discuss the advantages and disadvantages of the different types of housing pictured here. Asking them to think about these issues, however, helps to prepare them for the unit content.

Building and Using Vocabulary *(pages 104-105)*

30 mins

WARM-UP

- Divide the class into pairs of students. Ask partners to take turns talking about the place where they live now. Tell students to speak for at least one full minute.

- Model the warm-up activity by talking for one minute about the place where you live. Be sure to use simple language that students already know. For example: *I live far from here. It takes about 30 minutes to get here from my apartment. I live in a large apartment building, but my apartment is small. It has three rooms . . .*

Building Vocabulary

track 2-14 **Exercise A. | Using a Dictionary**

- Have students read the vocabulary words and check the words they already know.

- Play the audio so students can hear the vocabulary words.

- Give students time to look up any unfamiliar words in a dictionary.

Exercise B. | Have students complete the sentences individually before going over the answers as a class.

Answer Key

1. comfortable	5. stairs	9. walls
2. building	6. spacious	10. style
3. roof	7. balcony	
4. apartments	8. residents	

track 2-15 **Exercise C. |** This exercise introduces students to the architecture of Antoni Gaudí.

- Ask students to share any information they already know about Gaudí. (He lived from 1852 to 1926 and was from Barcelona, Spain.)

- Have students look at the photos and comment on the style of the buildings.

TIP You can handle exercise C in various ways. For example, make this a dictation exercise by playing the audio for each section separately and having students write the words as they hear them. You can also have students listen to the audio as they look at the photos, and then move on to the fill-in activity.

Answer Key

1. residents	5. apartments	9. stairs
2. building	6. spacious	10. comfortable
3. walls	7. balcony	
4. roof	8. style	

Using Vocabulary

Exercise A. | Discussion Have students look at the two additional examples of Gaudí's work and discuss the questions in pairs.

Exercise B. | Have students choose the correct vocabulary words in the context of the conversation.

Answer Key

apartment, spacious, style, balcony, roof, comfortable, stairs

Exercise C. | Have students practice the conversation from exercise **B** with a partner.

IDEAS FOR... **Expansion**

- Locate a Web site with additional photos of Gaudí's work to show students in class or have them research this information on their own. Ask students to bring in one image. Display the images around the classroom. Encourage students to share their opinion about Gaudí's buildings.

- Use the Internet to locate a brief educational video that shows Gaudí's buildings. Have students watch the video and write down a few opinions about Gaudí's work.

Pronunciation Note
(Antoni) Gaudí: **gow**-dee

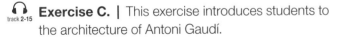

Developing Listening Skills

45 mins

(pages 106-107)

Before Listening

Using Context Clues | Go over the information in the box. Explain to students that learning strategies such as using context clues are tools that language learners can use to increase their success in a new language.

> **IDEAS FOR... Multi-level Classes**
>
> Take advantage of this opportunity to make a learning strategy explicit to your students. Lower-level learners especially will benefit from tools such as using context clues, recycling new vocabulary, and using the new language outside of class.

Exercise A.
track 2-16

- Play the audio and have students read along in the Student Book.

- Instruct partners to look for context clues in the conversation.

Answer Key *(Answers may vary.)*

Yes, but there's a lot of <u>congestion</u>.
Context clues: *everyone, park their cars, hard just to cross the street*
(The clues show that <u>congestion</u> refers to a busy area with a lot of people and cars.)

I like the <u>demographics</u> in Riverdale.
Context clues: *young families, good jobs*
(The clues show that <u>demographics</u> have to do with a group of people, e.g., their age and income level.)

True, but we're not <u>geriatric</u> yet.
Context clues: *getting older, children live on their own, still young enough*
(The clues show that <u>geriatric</u> has to do with being old or elderly.)

Then we'll ask the <u>real estate agent</u> . . .
Context clues: *show us apartments*
(The clues show that <u>real estate agent</u> is a person who helps you find or buy an apartment or house.)

Exercise B. | Have students practice the conversation in pairs.

Listening: A PowerPoint Presentation

Exercise A. | Listening for Main Ideas
track 2-17

> **Answer Key**
>
> b. There are nice apartments for sale in the new La Costa complex.

Exercise B. | Listening for Details Tell students that they will be listening for the numbers needed to fill in the blanks.
track 2-17

> **Answer Key** **1.** 22 **2.** 240 **3.** three **4.** four **5.** one

Exercise C. | Using Context Clues
track 2-17
Have students listen for context clues that could be helpful in understanding the underlined words.

> **Answer Key** *(Answers may vary.)*
>
> **1.** Context Clues: *you are real estate agents, we hope you bring many of them to see La Costa*
> (The clues tell us that <u>clients</u> are people that might want to buy an apartment or house.)
>
> **2.** Context Clues: *wall, art, colorful, pieces of glass, scene, beautiful*
> (The clues show that a <u>mosaic</u> is a type of art made of pieces of glass.)

After Listening

Critical Thinking | Have students form groups of three or four to discuss the questions. This exercise requires students to use higher-order thinking skills as they discuss the presentation they heard.

Exploring Spoken English

45 mins

(pages 108-110)

Grammar: Coordinating Conjunctions

IDEAS FOR...   Presenting Grammar

- Write the four pairs of sentences below in a column on the board:

    1. *I liked the large apartment.*
       I rented the small apartment.

    2. *She can live alone.*
       She can live with a roommate.

    3. *Sasha got a job in Moscow.*
       He is looking for an apartment there.

    4. *Jerry has a new car.*
       He likes it very much.

- In a column next to the sentences, write the coordinating conjunctions *and*, *but*, *or*, and *so*.

- Go over each pair of sentences. Then point to the coordinating conjunctions and ask students: *What is the relationship between these two sentences?*

- Have students tell you which coordinating conjunction corresponds with each pair of sentences. As students provide answers, draw lines from the sentence pairs to the correct coordinating conjunctions. (Answer Key: **1.** but **2.** or **3.** so **4.** and)

- Go over the information in the grammar box.

Exercise A. | Have students work in pairs to complete the exercise.

Answer Key

2. but, a contrast **3.** or, a choice **4.** but, a contrast
5. and, an addition **6.** so, a result

Exercise B. | Have students work individually to complete the sentences.

Answer Key *(Answers will vary.)*

2. I like my neighborhood, but there aren't any grocery stores nearby.
3. The building has friendly residents, and the apartments are spacious.
4. I can eat dinner at home, or I can go to a restaurant.
5. I love big cities, so I live in Sydney.
6. Apartments downtown are expensive, so I don't live there.

Exercise C. | Instruct partners to monitor the accuracy of one another's sentences, paying special attention to the use of the coordinating conjunctions.

Language Function: Agreeing and Disagreeing

Exercise A. | Go over the information in the box. Instruct students to use expressions for agreeing and disagreeing as they respond to their partner's statements.

track 2-18 **Exercise B. |** Have students underline the expressions for agreeing and disagreeing as they listen to and read the conversation.

Answer Key

Sasha: <u>That's a good point, but</u> I think the neighborhood is improving.

Janet: <u>I agree</u>.

Exercise C. | Have students practice the conversation from exercise **B** in pairs.

Exercise D. | Collaboration   Have partners look at the photos and work together to list several advantages of each place to live.

Exercise E. | Critical Thinking

- Go over the information in the Critical Thinking Focus box. You may also want to direct students to page 205 of the *Independent Student Handbook* for more information on the related topic of recognizing a speaker's bias.

- Have two sets of partners compare their lists of advantages.

- Ask each person in the group to decide which location from exercise **D** they would prefer to live in. Encourage students to give two or three reasons for their choice.

> **TIP**   As you go over the directions for exercise E, make sure students understand that it's a two-part activity. It may also be helpful to give time limits for each step.

Speaking *(page 111)*

30-45 mins

Expressing Relationships between Ideas

> **TIP**   You may want to review the information about coordinating conjunctions from page 108 before students begin exercise A.

Exercise A.

- Have partners take turns making statements about Dylan, the man in the photo.

- Students should connect two ideas—one from each side of the box—using a coordinating conjunction.

- After each statement, the speaker's partner must decide whether the statement makes sense or not.

Answer Key *(Answers may vary.)*

Sample answers:

Dylan loves music, so he plays the guitar.
Dylan works downtown, but he lives in the country.
Dylan is an excellent cook, but he eats at restaurants a lot.
Dylan often calls me, or he sends me emails.
Dylan has a car, but he takes a train to work.
Dylan works for an international company, so he travels to other countries a lot.

Exercise B.

- Go over the information in the Student to Student box about informal ways to show disagreement.

- Have partners identify the expressions for showing disagreement and then practice the conversation.

Answer Key

Hiroshi: <u>Are you sure about that?</u>
Hiroshi: <u>Hmm, I don't know . . .</u>

> **IDEAS FOR...   Checking Comprehension**
>
> Write a paragraph on the topic of housing. Use vocabulary and grammar that students are familiar with. The paragraph should include both correct and incorrect usage and punctuation of sentences with coordinating conjunctions. Make copies of the paragraph to hand out to the class. Have students correct the errors in the paragraph and hand in a revised paragraph for your review. Discuss suggested revisions as a class.

Viewing: Don't Believe Your Eyes! *(pages 112-113)*

30 mins

Overview of the Video | Between Naples and Salerno in western Italy, a rocky peninsula extends out into the sea. There, fishing villages with brightly painted houses are a reminder of Italy's past. One tradition being kept alive in the region is *trompe l'oeil* painting, which means "trick the eye" in French.

Before Viewing

Exercise A. | Self-Reflection   Have partners discuss the questions and explain which features make a house beautiful to them.

track 2-19

Exercise B. | Using a Dictionary

- Play the audio and have students read along in the Student Book.

- Give students time to look up the underlined words in a dictionary.

Exercise C. | Predicting Content   Based on the information they have read, have students check items they think they will learn about in the video.

While Viewing

> **IDEAS FOR...   Multi-level Classes**
>
> Show the video the first time with no sound and no captions. This allows students to concentrate on the visual content without the distraction of having a listening task to do. Add a language element by occasionally saying key words and phrases related to what students are seeing. (You may find it useful to refer to the video script on page 129 of this Teacher's Guide for this exercise.) Adding this language element provides input that is accessible to everyone in the class.

3:57
Exercise A. | Checking Predictions   Play the video again with the sound and with or without captions. Have students check the predictions they made in exercise **C**.

> ### Answer Key
>
> ✓ how artists learn to make *trompe l'oeil* paintings
>
> ✓ the history of *trompe l'oeil* painting in Camogli, Italy

3:57
Exercise B. | Play the video again. Have students circle the correct word or phrase in parentheses to complete each sentence.

> ### Answer Key
>
> **1.** Genoa **2.** 1700s **3.** grandmother **4.** Florence **5.** a full year **6.** history

After Viewing

Exercise A. | Discussion   Have students think about and respond to the video in small groups.

Exercise B. | Critical Thinking   As a bridge between the video and Lesson B, small groups discuss the quotation and the question that follows.

Building and Using Vocabulary *(pages 114-115)*

30 mins

WARM-UP

- Write an amount of money on the board that would be sufficient to take a family of four on a nice vacation anywhere in the world (e.g., $10,000).

- Tell students: *Use your imagination. You have $10,000, and you want to go on a vacation with your family.* Ask students questions such as: *Where do you want to go? What do you want to do?* List students' ideas on the board.

- Tell students that in this section, they will learn about a place where vacation homes are popular. In other words, people have enough money for a second home, and they buy a house that they can visit on every vacation.

Building Vocabulary

> **TIP** Students may or may not have much real-world experience with vacations and travel. If possible, show students a few promotional tourism videos from a video-sharing Web site. These will provide ideas for the discussion activities.

 track 2-20 **Exercise A. | Using a Dictionary**

- Have students read the vocabulary words and check the words they already know.

- Play the audio so students can hear the vocabulary words.

> **IDEAS FOR...** Checking Comprehension
>
> To gauge how difficult the new set of vocabulary words is for students, ask them to tell you a word they checked. Then ask them what it means, or ask them to use the word in a sentence.

Exercise B. | Have students use a dictionary to match the vocabulary words to the definitions.

Answer Key

1. build	5. property	9. rapid
2. especially	6. locations	10. belong
3. tourists	7. population	
4. deserts	8. damage	

Exercise C. | Discussion   Have partners discuss their travel preferences for an imaginary vacation.

Using Vocabulary

track 2-21

- Give students time to read the article and fill in the blanks.

- Play the audio and have students check their answers.

- Ask students to talk about other areas that are popular vacation destinations. Have students brainstorm a few ideas about why these areas are popular.

Answer Key

1. locations	5. belong	9. build
2. tourists	6. especially	10. damage
3. deserts	7. population	
4. property	8. rapid	

45 mins

Developing Listening Skills
(pages 116-117)

track 2-22

Pronunciation: Contractions with *Be*

In English, grammatical information can often be found in word endings—from plural and possessive forms to the past participle and gerund forms. Tell students that paying attention to word endings while listening is a useful way to increase comprehension.

- Go over the information in the box.

- Play the audio so students can hear the examples.

- Emphasize that adding a contracted form of *be* does not change the number of syllables in a word.

Answer Key   2. That's 3. He's 4. I'm 5. You're 6. There's

Before Listening

Prior Knowledge | Using the map, photo, and their prior knowledge, students might be able to answer all of the questions correctly. It's also fine if they make a guess. Have students decide if each statement is true or false. Then have students check their answers on page 117.

Answer Key

1. F (It's in several countries.) 2. T 3. T
4. T (if they bring in water)

Listening: A Conversation

track 2-23

Exercise A. | Listening for Main Ideas

- Give students time to read the questions and answer choices.

- Play the audio. Have students choose the correct answers.

Answer Key   1. b 2. c 3. a

track 2-23

Exercise B. | Listening for Details

- Give students time to read the sentences from the listening passage.

- Play the audio. Instruct students to fill in the blanks with the word or phrase that they hear.

Answer Key   1. population 2. It's 3. That's
4. property 5. belongs

After Listening

Critical Thinking

- Have students use their own words to tell their partner about the government plan they heard about in the listening passage.

- The Critical Thinking exercise involves paraphrasing— communicating someone else's ideas using one's own words. Paraphrasing requires a variety of skills, but understanding the information and knowing some synonyms are perhaps the most relevant skills. To prepare students for the exercise, remind them of synonyms they already know as you discuss the listening passage. For example:

T: That's right, they're selling <u>property</u> there at a low price. What kind of property? Do you think they're selling <u>buildings</u> or <u>land</u>?

S: I think land. They're "greening" land so that farmers can grow food there and people can go and live there. They're not selling buildings.

Exploring Spoken English

(pages 118-119)

30 mins

WARM-UP

Using straw, grass, and other plants to construct buildings is a very old idea. Some modern-day builders have rediscovered this construction technique, which is both economical and environmentally friendly.

- Point out the photo of the interior of a house on page 119. Tell students that the house is made of an unusual material.

track 2-24

Exercise A.

- Play the audio and have students read along in the Student Book.
- Discuss the question in the first line of the article as a class.
- Give students time to reread the article at their own pace.
- Answer any questions students have.

Exercise B. | Discussion Have students discuss the questions in pairs.

> **TIP** The title of the article and exercise B contain the expression *go green*. Explain that when we *go green*, we do things that are good for the environment, for example, by using less electricity or not using plastic bags.

Grammar: Time Relationships in the Simple Present Tense

> **IDEAS FOR... Presenting Grammar**
>
> - Direct students' attention to the grammar box on page 108. Ask: *Why do we use coordinating conjunctions?* (to connect sentences and show relationships between ideas)
> - Write these words on the board: *when, after, before, while, until*
> - Ask students: *What are all of these words about?* or *What kind of relationships will we talk about today?* (time)
> - Go over the information in the box.

Exercise A.

Answer Key *(Answers will vary.)*

Sample answers:

2. After the straw is tied together in bales, people stack the bales.
3. When people finish stacking the bales to make walls, they apply plaster.
4. After the plaster dries, people paint it.
5. People can live in the house when it is finished.

Exercise B. | Have partners share their sentences from exercise **A**.

Exercise C. | Have partners work together to complete each sentence with their own ideas.

Answer Key *(Answers will vary.)*

Sample answers:

2. It's important to ask questions about an apartment before you rent it.
3. When I have a question, I usually talk to my teacher.
4. Good students study for a test until they know all of the material well.
5. After they get married, many people buy new furniture.
6. I like to listen to music while I study.

Exercise D. | Have students share their sentences from exercise **C** in small groups.

45 mins

Engage: Role-Playing a Meeting with Real Estate Agents *(page 120)*

WARM-UP

In this activity, students have the opportunity to role-play two different people—a real estate agent and a client.

- Write *real estate agent* on the board, or if you have a projector in class, show students a photo of a real estate agent doing his or her job.

- Ask students: *Do you remember the real estate agents from Lesson A? What was their job?* (to show clients properties to buy)

- Go over the information about role-playing in the Presentation Skills box at the bottom of the page.

Exercise A.

- Go over the information at the top of page 120.

- Have students choose one kind of property from the list.

Exercise B. | Brainstorming
Instruct students to work together to create a list of "wants."

> **TIP** Ask students to choose one partner to act as secretary and write down the items in the list.

Exercise C. | Critical Thinking
Just as they did on page 110 in Lesson A, students need to decide what is most important to them in their property.

Exercise D. | Role-Playing

- Go over the directions and give time limits.

- Ask for two student volunteers to read the speech bubbles aloud.

- Tell students to follow the instructions to complete the activity.

> **TIP** If you don't have an even number of pairs in the class, ask a pair of your more advanced students to do the role-play by themselves, with one person acting as the agent and one as the client. Then they can switch roles.

> **TIP** Since all of the students will be doing their role-plays at the same time, walk around the classroom and take notes on things you notice. Then at the end of the activity, give the class general feedback on things such as eye contact and language usage.

IDEAS FOR... Expansion

If possible, ask a guest speaker whose job is related to real estate or housing to visit your class. The guest simply has to talk about his or her job. Ask students to prepare for the guest speaker by writing down some questions they would like to ask the guest ahead of time. On the day the speaker visits, make sure that he or she has a chance to ask the students questions, too.

Exploring Space

Academic Track
Interdisciplinary

Academic Pathways:

Lesson A: Listening to a Presentation by a
Medical Doctor
Talking about the Future

Lesson B: Listening to a Talk by a Tour Guide
Planning a Trip to an Astronomical Site

Unit Theme

Unit 7 looks at several kinds of space exploration with a focus on some of the technology that allows people to view space, live in space, and send unmanned probes out into space.

Unit 7 is about the topic of space exploration as it relates to:
– space stations
– travel to Mars
– space probes
– telescopes
– the dark-sky movement

Think and Discuss *(page 121)*

5 mins

Although very few people will ever travel or work in space as the astronaut in this photo does, most of us do look up into the night sky and think about the things we see—the sun, moon, and stars.

- Discuss the questions.

- Encourage students to respond to the photograph and to use the information on this page to preview the content of the unit.

Exploring the Theme: Exploring Space *(pages 122-123)*

15 mins

The opening spread features a photo from the Hubble Space Telescope as well as key vocabulary from the unit.

- Point out the large photograph and caption and make sure students know that it shows a *galaxy* (an enormous group of stars) far from the earth, and that a *telescope* (an instrument for seeing far away) was used to take the photo.

- Go through the Exploring the Theme questions and discuss the other photos and captions. Students should understand that although space exploration began with only two countries—the former Soviet Union and the United States—it is now a much more international endeavor.

> TIP Discuss the topics of the three smaller photos on page 122 in chronological order: satellites, the first moon landing, and space agencies.

IDEAS FOR...   Expansion

Ask students to draw a time line and label the time line with the events from page 122. (Refer students to page 215 of the *Independent Student Handbook* for more information on time lines.) Encourage students to add more information about space exploration to their time lines as they work through the unit.

30 mins

Building and Using Vocabulary *(pages 124-125)*

WARM-UP

- Write the words *astronaut* and *cosmonaut* on the board and ask students if they know what the words mean.

- Explain that these people (*astronauts* in the United States or *cosmonauts* in Russia) travel to space and work in space.

- Ask students to find an astronaut/cosmonaut in the photos on these pages.

Building Vocabulary

 track 2-25 **Exercise A. | Using a Dictionary**

- Have students read the vocabulary words and check the words they already know.

- Play the audio so students can hear the vocabulary words.

- Give students time to look up any words they're not sure about in a dictionary.

track 2-26 **Exercise B. | Meaning from Context**
Students get a second look at the Lesson A vocabulary in the context of an article about astronaut Don Thomas' experiences in space.

- Play the audio and have students read along in the Student Book.

- Give students time to read the article a second time at their own pace.

Exercise C. | Instruct each partner to explain one of the two topics from the article.

> **Answer Key** *(Student responses will vary.)*
>
> **Student A:** He talks about the colors because stars look different from space. Stars of different colors look more amazing than the all-white stars we see from Earth.
>
> **Student B:** Stars appear to twinkle because their light passes through the earth's atmosphere, and gases in the atmosphere are always moving.

> **IDEAS FOR...** Checking Comprehension
>
> The fourth and fifth paragraphs in the article on page 124 describe the life cycle of our own sun—from its birth to its eventual death. To engage your visual learners, have students draw a diagram of the process with a partner. Then ask volunteers to draw their diagram on the board and explain it to the class.

TIP Refer back to the fourth paragraph in the article in exercise B. Ask students to tell you how many syllables are in each word with an *-ed* ending: *formed (1), called (1), collapsed (2), heated (2).* If necessary, have students review the pronunciation box on page 46.

Using Vocabulary

Exercise A. | Have students complete the sentences individually. Then go over the answers as a class.

> **Answer Key**
>
> | | | |
> |---|---|---|
> | 1. amazing | 5. gravity | 9. ago |
> | 2. appears | 6. In contrast | 10. become |
> | 3. atmosphere | 7. even | |
> | 4. gas | 8. lasted | |

Exercise B. | Prior Knowledge Have students discuss the questions in pairs.

Developing Listening Skills

45 mins *(pages 126-127)*

Pronunciation: Contractions with *Will*

track 2-27

Listening for word endings in English is essential for accurate comprehension. In this section, students practice saying and hearing contractions with pronouns and *will* when talking about the future.

- Go over the information in the box.
- Play the audio so students can hear the examples.

Exercise A. | Play the audio and instruct students to listen and repeat.

track 2-28

Exercise B. | Have students practice saying the sentences in pairs.

> **TIP** The pronunciation section is a preview of the Lesson A grammar. If students have questions now about using *will*, ask them to hold their questions until you get to the Exploring Spoken English section on page 128.

Before Listening

Predicting Content | Have pairs of students make predictions about the audio. Encourage students to look at the photo and title on page 127 for clues.

> **Answer Key** *(Predictions may vary.)*
>
> The first three topics are about health and the human body. The doctor will probably not discuss the fourth topic since it does not relate to health effects of space travel.

Listening: A Presentation by a Medical Doctor

Exercise A. | Checking Predictions

track 2-29

Have students listen and check the predictions from the Before Listening activity.

Exercise B. | Listening for Main Ideas

track 2-29

- Give students time to read the questions and the answer choices.
- Play the audio. Have students choose the correct answers.

> **Answer Key**   **1.** c **2.** c **3.** a **4.** b

Exercise C. | Making Inferences

track 2-29

- Give students time to read the statements.
- Play the audio. Have students decide if the statements are true or false based on the information they infer from the audio.

> **TIP** Have students take brief notes while listening to Track 2-29. Then ask students to use their notes to help them with the statements in exercise C. Go over the answers as a class and ask students to refer to their notes to explain their answers (See suggestions in the Answer Key below).

> **Answer Key**
>
> 1. F (He says he always enjoys talking to children.)
> 2. T (He spent a month on a space station.)
> 3. T (He says it might not taste as good as fresh food.)
> 4. F (He says that you need two or three hours of exercise every day in space.)

After Listening

Exercise A. | Collaboration   Partners work together to create a one-day schedule for an imaginary astronaut using information from the listening passage.

Exercise B. | Critical Thinking   Have students compare their schedules from exercise **A** in small groups.

45 mins

Exploring Spoken English
(pages 128-130)

Grammar: Future Time—*Will* and *Be Going To*

IDEAS FOR... Presenting Grammar

- Write the word *learn* on the board. Ask students: *What's the simple past tense of* learn? (learned) Add the *-ed* ending.
- Now erase the *-ed* ending and write the following example sentences on the board: *I will learn to speak French someday. The class is going to learn about French cooking on Friday.*
- Ask students: *What's the difference between these two sentences? When do we use* will *and* be going to?
- Go over the information in the grammar box.

Exercise A. | Have students underline *will* and *be going to* in the conversation before they practice it with a partner.

Answer Key

Raymond: How <u>are you going to</u> change it?

Kiki: Well, <u>I'm still going to</u> talk about life on the space station . . . But <u>I'll</u> add information about future research on the station.

Raymond: That sounds interesting. What kind of research <u>are they going to</u> do?

Kiki: Sure, but the research projects <u>will</u> be even more international in the future.

Raymond: So astronauts from different countries <u>will</u> work together more?

Exercise B. | Have students use their own ideas to answer the questions with their partner.

> **Answer Key** *(Answers will vary.)*

track 2-30

Exercise C. | Have students listen to the audio and read along in the Student Book. Then have students underline *will* and *be going to*.

Answer Key

Dr. Takei: . . . If astronauts go to Mars, <u>they'll</u> need spacesuits to stay warm. . . Those spacesuits <u>will</u> need to provide oxygen and air pressure, too.

Dr. Takei: . . . if you add a few things to it, <u>it's going to</u> begin to warm the planet.

Dr. Takei: However, oxygen <u>is still going to</u> be a problem. Some scientists think that future astronauts <u>will</u> bring plants to Mars to make oxygen. . .

Interviewer: <u>Will</u> any of this really happen?

Dr. Takei: In my opinion, it <u>won't</u> happen during our lives, or any time soon.

TIP As you discuss the conversation on page 128 and the interview on page 129, point out that both *will* and *be going to* are used to speak in a general way about the future. In the conversation, the speaker also uses both forms to talk about planned events.

Exercise D. | Critical Thinking In small groups, have students discuss the questions, which encourage them to think about the content of the interview on page 129.

Language Function: Making Predictions

Go over the information in the box. Tell students that making predictions involves considering the information that we know now and using our judgment to say what we think will happen in the future.

Exercise A. | Have students work individually to complete the sentences.

Answer Key *(Answers will vary.)*

Sample Answers:

2. be much larger **3.** travel to Mars **4.** be much smaller **5.** come from new sources **6.** see a lot of changes in the world

Exercise B.

- Go over the information in the Student to Student box.

- Have students share and discuss their predictions from exercise **A**.

- Encourage students to use the expressions from the box and to give reasons for their ideas.

Speaking *(page 131)*

30-45 mins

Talking about the Future

The activities on page 131 move away from the topic of space exploration and give students a chance to talk about their own hopes and plans for the future.

Exercise A. | The time line shows present and future events in John's life. (Events in the present start at the left). Have students use the information from the time line to complete the sentences.

Answer Key

1. is taking classes **2.** is going to take his final exams **3.** is going to graduate **4.** is going to move back to Europe **5.** will get married and have children

Exercise B. | Have students practice saying the sentences they wrote in exercise **A** with a partner.

Exercise C. | Self-Reflection Have students check the items they would like to do in the future.

Exercise D.

- Go over the information and example sentences in the Presentation Skills box.

- Have students tell their partner about their hopes and plans for the future.

- Encourage students to use expressions from the box to indicate when they think things will happen in the future.

Viewing: Exploration of the Solar System *(pages 132-133)*

30 mins

Overview of the Video | In 1961, Yuri Gagarin became the first person to orbit the earth in a spacecraft. Since then, manned space exploration has gotten a lot of attention—from moon landings to space walks outside the International Space Station. Unmanned space exploration also has an important role to play, especially when long distances are involved. Unmanned space probes can go places where no human being has been able to go.

Before Viewing

Exercise A. | Critical Thinking Have students work in pairs to generate ideas for the T-chart.

TIP After students have discussed the T-chart in pairs, copy the T-chart on the board and elicit ideas from the class.

 Exercise B. | Using a Dictionary
track 2-31

- Play the audio and have students read along in the Student Book.
- Give students time to look up the underlined words in a dictionary.

While Viewing

 Exercise A.
2:21

- Go over the directions and the names for the planets.
- Play the video with no captions. Have students watch and check the names of the planets they hear.

Answer Key All of the planets except Earth are mentioned in the video.

 Exercise B. | Have students watch the video again and match the name of each planet to the probe or probes that studied it.
2:21

Answer Key 1. b 2. e 3. a 4. c, f 5. d 6. c, f 7. f 8. f

After Viewing

Critical Thinking | As a bridge between Lesson A and Lesson B, have students discuss the questions in small groups.

IDEAS FOR... Expansion

The topic of space exploration often involves technical language, which can make Internet research difficult for language learners. The National Aeronautics and Space Administration (NASA) Web site, however, contains a special section that includes videos, slide shows, and other features that are appropriate for independent study.

- Look through the Web site yourself first to find out where to direct your students.
- Create a worksheet or other task for students to do when they visit the Web site.

Pronunciation Note
Yuri Gagarin: **your**-ee gah-**gar**-in

Building and Using Vocabulary *(pages 134-135)*

30 mins

WARM-UP

- Write the word *telescope* on the board. Ask: *What can you do with a telescope?* (see distant objects in space)

- Remind students of the unit theme and ask: *How do we use telescopes in space exploration?* Encourage the class to brainstorm some ideas.

Building Vocabulary

track 2-32

Exercise A. | Meaning from Context

- Preview the article by briefly discussing the section titles and the photographs.

- Give students time to read the article and see the vocabulary words in context.

Using Vocabulary

Exercise B.

- Have students write each vocabulary word next to its definition.

- As you go over the answers, ask students to identify context clues in the reading.

Answer Key

1. necessary	5. completely	9. view
2. among	6. discovered	10. size
3. invented	7. reach	
4. observe	8. reflect	

IDEAS FOR... Checking Comprehension

Draw a blank time line on the board. (Refer to page 215 of the *Independent Student Handbook* for an example.) Alongside the time line, write the headings *past, present,* and *future*. Conduct a brief class discussion of the reading on page 134. Ask questions to elicit information from students, and fill in the time line based on their answers. For example:

T: Let's start with the past. In the reading, what two people were important to the history of the telescope?

S: Galileo and Isaac Newton.

T: Good, and what did Galileo do?

TIP Some students will volunteer answers during a class discussion, while others will not. Be sure to call on the quiet students so that everyone in the class participates.

Exercise C. | Instruct students to choose the correct vocabulary word for each sentence.

Answer Key   1. size 2. reflects 3. necessary 4. discovered 5. among

Exercise D. | Have students take the multiple-choice "Astronomy Quiz," which is related to telescopes. If students are unsure of an answer, instruct them to make a prediction or their best guess.

Answer Key   1. b 2. b 3. a 4. b

TIP The purpose of the quiz is to recycle target vocabulary and help prepare students for the upcoming listening passage.

Developing Listening Skills

45 mins

(pages 136-137)

WARM-UP

- If your classroom has Internet access, show students the Web site of the Yerkes Observatory—especially the photographs of the building found in the image gallery.

- Ask students to guess where the observatory is and how old it is.

Before Listening

Listening for Time Expressions | Go over the information in the box. Students may already be familiar with the time expressions presented in this section, but they may not be sure how to use the expressions correctly. This section presents the expressions in an unusual way, showing students the grammatical functions the time expressions can perform.

Exercise A. | Have students listen for time expressions in an excerpt of the main listening passage.

Answer Key

- ✓ before
- ✓ first
- ✓ next

Exercise B. | Have students work in pairs to complete each sentence by choosing the best time expression in parentheses. Make sure students practice reading the sentences aloud.

Answer Key 1. before 2. as soon as 3. last
4. during 5. After 6. Finally

Listening: A Talk by a Tour Guide

Exercise A. | **Listening for Main Ideas**

- Give students time to read the statements and answer choices.

- Play the audio. Have students listen and choose the correct answers.

Answer Key 1. b 2. c 3. c

Exercise B. | **Note-Taking** Teaching note-taking skills can be a challenge. This exercise uses partially completed notes to illustrate clear, brief, and well-organized notes. Have students listen to the audio again and complete the notes.

Answer Key (18)90s, mirrors, 40, country

After Listening

Critical Thinking | In small groups, have students expand on the information from the listening passage by discussing the questions.

> **TIP** In the Critical Thinking exercise, students need to think about how the world has changed since the Yerkes Observatory was built in the 1890s. For example, major observatories are now built far from city lights. The Yerkes site is not away from city lights.

IDEAS FOR... Expansion

If possible, take your class on a guided tour of an observatory or planetarium. Or, ask students who have visited an observatory or planetarium to share their own experiences. Students give a short summary to the class or small groups.

Exploring Spoken English
(pages 138-139)

30 mins

Grammar: Future Time—The Present Continuous and the Simple Present Forms

- Review *will* and *be going to* for talking about the future. Ask students several questions using the two forms. For example:

  T: Jean, what <u>are you going to do</u> after class?
  S: <u>I'm going to walk</u> to the library after class.
  T: Good. Marisol, what time <u>will</u> you eat dinner tonight?

- Tell students that they will learn two more ways to talk about the future.

- Go over the information in the box.

Exercise A.

Answer Key

2. leaves (is leaving) 3. is giving 4. are getting
5. starts (is starting) 6. begins

TIP For scheduled events such as items 2 and 5 of exercise A, English speakers more often use the simple present over the present continuous. Both answers, however, are correct.

Exercise B. | Using a Dictionary
track 2-35

Exercise **B** provides background information for the activities on page 139. Play the audio as students read along in the Student Book. Have them look up any new words they think are important in a dictionary.

TIP After students finish exercise B, discuss some of the words that they decided to look up. Ask them why they thought the words were important.

Exercise C. | Have students underline the
track 2-36
sentences that contain the present continuous or simple present form to refer to the future.

Answer Key

Tim: Well, <u>they're going</u> to a national park. It's far from any cities.

Tim: The bus <u>leaves</u> at five o'clock on Friday afternoon, and it <u>gets</u> to the park around seven thirty.

Yoshi: What time does the bus <u>get</u> back here?

Tim: It <u>gets</u> back pretty late—around midnight.

Exercise D. | Have students practice the conversation in pairs.

Critical Thinking Focus: Discussing Pros and Cons

- Go over the information in the Critical Thinking Focus box.

- In small groups, have students discuss the ideas in the chart and add their own ideas.

IDEAS FOR... **Multi-level Classes**

This Critical Thinking activity works well with multi-level groups because it provides linguistic input (the language in the chart) for students to use in discussion. As students add their own ideas, they can do so at their own language level.

Engage: Planning a Trip to an Astronomical Site *(page 140)*

45 mins

WARM-UP

Lesson B of this unit has focused on ways that people on Earth can connect with space, for example by using a telescope or going someplace dark to see the night sky. In this activity, small groups need to choose among three possible destinations for an astronomy-themed trip.

- Remind students of information they learned about space exploration in this unit.
- Go over the information at the top of page 140.
- Point out the photos of the three astronomy-related sites.

Exercise A.

- Have students read about the three sites on their own.
- Go over the information at the top of the page.
- Give students time to read about the three sites.

TIP You can begin this activity by putting students into pairs first. Have each pair of students read about each site. Then split the pairs and put students in small groups. Have each student tell the other group members about what they have read.

Exercise B. | Discussion   In small groups, have students decide which site to visit. Since the sites are in different parts of the world, encourage students to think about all related factors including travel costs from your location.

Exercise C. | Planning a Presentation   In small groups, students discuss where they will go and how they will present their decision to another group.

- Remind students that considering pros and cons is an important part of critical thinking. Encourage them to think of advantages and disadvantages for each hypothetical trip.

- Have students take brief notes on their discussion—especially on the reasons for their decision.

Exercise D. | Presentation   Have each small group give a presentation to another small group of students.

TIP During the presentations, walk around the classroom and take notes so that you can give general feedback to the class as a wrap-up activity. Focus on how well students have explained their choice.

Academic Track
Art/Music

Academic Pathways:

Lesson A: Listening to a PowerPoint Presentation
Discussing Ideas about Photographs

Lesson B: Listening to a Radio Program
Giving a Group Presentation

Unit Theme

Art and music are found in every culture, and most cultures have evidence of art and music traditions that span thousands of years of history.

Unit 8 discusses art and music as it relates to:

– temporary forms of art
– paintings by elephants
– graffiti

– ukulele music
– folk dancing

5
mins

Think and Discuss *(page 141)*

Discuss the questions as a class. If students have trouble answering question 2, you can help them articulate their ideas by asking the following questions: *When do you like to listen to music? What kind of music do you like? Why? Do you have a favorite artist? Do you like the art in the hallway outside this classroom? Why, or why not?*

15
mins

Exploring the Theme: Art and Music *(pages 142-143)*

The opening spread features a large mural by Diego Rivera and smaller photos showing a child's chalk drawings, a stone sculpture, and a performer doing traditional folk dancing from Indonesia.

The mural, called *Detroit Industry*, is just one of the murals Rivera painted at the Detroit Institute of Arts in 1932 and 1933. It was commissioned by Edsel Ford, and it depicts workers in a large factory similar to the automobile factories in Detroit at that time.

■ Discuss the questions. If students need help answering question 3, ask: *Do you like to look at paintings? Do you enjoy painting or drawing pictures?*

IDEAS FOR... **Expansion**

Conduct a class discussion of the mural on pages 142 and 143. (If you have a large class, you may alternatively choose to assign one or two questions for small-group discussions.) Discussion questions could include the following:

1. What do you see in the mural? What do you notice about the workers?
2. What does the mural say about life in the United States in the 1930s?
3. Do you think the images in the mural are realistic? Do they look like people in real life?
4. How is a large mural different from a smaller painting? Do they have different purposes or different effects?

Building and Using Vocabulary *(pages 144-145)*

30 mins

WARM-UP

The sculptures of Jason deCaires Taylor have received a lot of attention. His work includes striking portrayals of ordinary people. His subjects are usually positioned in large groups. And most interestingly, they're underwater—off the coasts of Mexico, Grenada, and Greece, among other places.

- Direct students' attention to the photos on these pages and have them read the captions.

- Make sure students understand the word *sculpture*. Refer back to its usage in the opening spread on pages 142 and 143.

- Ask students why they think the sculptures are underwater.

Building Vocabulary

track 3-2 Exercise A. | Using a Dictionary

- Have students read the vocabulary words and check the words they already know.

- Play the audio so students can hear the vocabulary words.

Exercise B. | Instruct students to use a dictionary as needed to complete the definitions.

Answer Key

1. sculptures	5. repeat	9. conscious of
2. public	6. solid	10. constantly
3. temporary	7. forever	
4. huge	8. copies	

Exercise C. | Discussion   As students discuss the questions in pairs, have them focus on expressing personal opinions while recycling target vocabulary words.

track 3-3 Using Vocabulary

- Have students read the article and fill in the blanks with the correct vocabulary words from page 144.

- Play the audio and have students check their answers.

Answer Key

1. solid	5. public	9. temporary
2. conscious of	6. huge	10. forever
3. sculptures	7. repeat	
4. copies	8. constantly	

IDEAS FOR...   Checking Comprehension

Write these *wh-* question words on the board: *who, what, where, when,* and *why.* Ask students questions about the reading passage:

1. Who made these sculptures? Who is the artist?
2. What sort of sculptures does this artist make?
3. Where are these sculptures?
4. Why are the sculptures underwater?
5. When can people see the sculptures? (For how long?)

Pronunciation Note
(Jason) deCaires (Taylor): dee-**carries**

Developing Listening Skills

(pages 146-147)

45
mins

Before Listening

Taking Notes While Listening.

- Go over the information in the box.

- Ask students about their experiences with note-taking, especially in English. Encourage students to refer to pages 206 and 207 of the *Independent Student Handbook* for more information on improving note-taking skills.

Using a Dictionary | Have students answer the questions individually.

> **Answer Key** *(Answers may vary.)*
>
> **1.** an eraser **2.** the beach **3.** for writing or drawing

TIP Tell students that the Using a Dictionary exercise provides useful vocabulary that they will need while they listen and take notes in the upcoming Listening section.

Listening: A PowerPoint Presentation

track 3-4

Exercise A. | Note-Taking

This exercise provides partially completed notes in outline form. Play the audio and have students complete the notes on pages 146 and 147.

> **Answer Key**
>
> (Slide #1) Location: **Montreal, Canada**
>   2. **brings people together**
> (Slide #2) Location: **Madrid, Spain**
>   Type of art: **chalk art**
> (Slide #3) Location: **California, USA**
>   Type of art: **sand art**
> (Slide #4) Time to finish a piece: **7 hours**
>   Reason art is temporary: **Ocean tides erase the art**

track 3-4
Exercise B. | Play the audio a second time for students to hear the lecture excerpt again and check their notes from exercise **A**.

After Listening

Exercise A. | Discussion In small groups, have students discuss the questions about temporary art.

TIP Give students a time limit for the small-group discussion.

Exercise B. | Critical Thinking

- Ask students what they see in the photo at the bottom of page 147.

- Give students time to read the information.

- Have students discuss the questions in small groups.

> **Answer Key** *(Answers will vary.)*
>
> For questions 2 and 3, students might say that the Internet or the library is a good place to find this information.

TIP Keep students in the same small groups for exercises A and B in this After Listening section.

IDEAS FOR... **Expansion**

- Have students do research on their own to find the title of the book mentioned in exercise **B**.

- Have students find more photos of Beever's work. They should take notes on their reaction to the art and bring in a photo to share in class.

Exploring Spoken English
(pages 148-150)

45 mins

Grammar: Modals of Possibility and Probability

> ### IDEAS FOR... Presenting Grammar
>
> ■ Write these two sentences on the board: *It's possible. It's probable.*
>
> ■ With students, come up with appropriate sentences to illustrate the difference between possibility and probability. For example:
>
> **T:** It will rain tonight. (pointing to the board) What do you think? It's possible, or it's probable?
>
> **S:** It's possible. I mean, the forecast doesn't call for rain tonight, but who knows?
>
> **T:** Good. Now, what's something that is probable?
>
> **S:** We'll have another quiz pretty soon.
>
> **T:** You're right! That's probable—it's likely to happen. We'll probably have a quiz next week, or maybe the week after.
>
> ■ Go over the information in the box.

Exercise A. (track 3-5)

■ Play the audio and have students read along in the Student Book.

■ Have students identify and underline the modals of possibility and probability in the conversations.

Answer Key

Conversation 1
Amy: She <u>must be</u> out of town . . .
Bill: Right—she <u>could be</u> in Osaka.

Conversation 2
Jenna: He <u>might be</u> Ann's father . . .
Reggie: No, he <u>can't be</u> Ann's father.

Jenna: We <u>could go</u> over there . . .
Reggie: Yes, but he <u>might not want</u> to talk to us now.

Exercise B. | Have students practice the two conversations from exercise **A** in pairs.

> **TIP** Talk about the picture and caption on page 148 after you complete the exercises on page 149.

Language Function: Speculating about a Situation

Go over the information in the box and explain to students that different grammatical structures can be used to talk about possibility and probability, including modals and the adverbs *perhaps* and *maybe*.

> **TIP** You might want to discuss the information in the Language Function box after students complete exercise A.

Exercise A. (track 3-6)

■ Play the audio and have students read along in the Student Book. Alternatively, have students read the article silently without the audio.

■ Have students identify the correct modals of possibility and probability in the article.

Answer Key   1. might 2. might 3. could 4. may

Exercise B. | In small groups, have students practice the language function while discussing the topic of elephant paintings.

Exercise C. | Critical Thinking   Have students discuss the questions in small groups. Encourage them to move beyond the material in the Student Book.

Exercise D.

- Instruct students to read about the three artists.

- Have small groups generate questions about the artists and speculate about the answers.

> **IDEAS FOR...   Multi-level Classes**
>
> In the activities on page 150, students do extensive work in small groups. Changing the composition of the groups once or twice allows students to work with more of their classmates and prevents some of the frustration that higher-level students may feel during group work.

 Speaking *(page 151)*

30-45 mins

Discussing Ideas about Photographs

Exercise A. | Have students practice the conversation with a partner.

Exercise B. | Instruct students to have their own conversations about the two remaining photos, speculating on what the photos might be and using language for talking about possibility and probability.

> **TIP**   The goal of exercise B is to have engaging discussion, but students may still be curious about the photos after talking about them. If this is the case, give them the following information about the three photos on this page: (from top to bottom) *This is a photo of a tooth from an extinct mammoth as seen under a microscope. This is a photo of a cross-section of a bamboo fishing pole as seen under a microscope. This is a close-up photo of bird feathers.*

Exercise C. | Collaboration   Have partners choose one of the photos they discussed in exercise **B** and complete the conversation about it.

Exercise D. | Role-Playing   Have students join another pair to present their conversations from exercise **C**. Go over the Presentation Skills box before student begin the role-play.

> **TIP**   After students complete exercise D, have them practice the other pair's conversation in addition to their own.

> **IDEAS FOR...   Checking Comprehension**
>
> The phrase *may be* can be easy to confuse with the adverb *maybe*. To find out whether your students understand the difference, write this example sentence on the board and have students choose the correct word or phrase:
>
> *I can't find my book. It (1) maybe/may be at my apartment, or (2) maybe/may be I left it on the bus.*
>
> (**Answer Key: 1.** may be **2.** maybe)

Viewing: Urban Art

30 mins

(pages 152-153)

Overview of the Video | Graffiti artists such as Nick Posada are usually not discussed in the same breath as artists whose work is exhibited in fine art galleries. But in Washington, D.C., one gallery owner sees graffiti—the colorful outdoor art of the street—as a fresh form of pop art. At his gallery, collectors are willing to spend money on the kind of artwork that some people in urban areas consider ugly.

Before Viewing

Exercise A. | Discussion Have students discuss the questions in pairs.

> **TIP** Make sure students understand the terms *graffiti* and *pop art,* both of which are illustrated in the photos on these pages.

Exercise B. | Meaning from Context
Instruct students to use context clues to figure out the meanings of the underlined words.

> **IDEAS FOR... Checking Comprehension**
>
> After students finish exercise **B**, go over the information as a class and ask students to identify the context clues that helped them understand the underlined words.

Exercise C. | As students work in pairs, have them recycle the new vocabulary from exercise **B** while they complete the T-chart that outlines key concepts from the video.

Answer Key

Traditional Art
gallery, commissioned, respected

Graffiti
spontaneous, inventive

Exercise D. | Critical Thinking Have students discuss the questions in pairs.

> **TIP** Students will hear the saying "Beauty is in the eye of the beholder" from exercise D in the video. Consequently, the Critical Thinking task prepares students for both the language and the ideas in the video.

While Viewing

2:08

Exercise A.

- Play the video with or without the captions.

- As students watch the video, have them complete the chart.

Exercise B. | Discussion Have students discuss their answers from exercise **A** in pairs.

2:08 **Exercise C. |** As students watch the video a second time, instruct them to listen specifically for the underlined words from page 152. Play the video with no captions.

After Viewing

Critical Thinking | Have students discuss the questions in pairs.

> **TIP** Ask students to look at all of the photos on pages 152 and 153 and also to think about the graffiti in the video as they discuss the Critical Thinking questions.

Building and Using Vocabulary *(pages 154-155)*

30 mins

WARM-UP

- Play a piece of music in class—preferably something that won't be familiar to students.

- Have students take notes on their thoughts and feelings as they listen to the music.

- Conduct a brief class discussion about the music you played and about music in general.

Building Vocabulary

track 3-7

Exercise A. | Using a Dictionary

- Have students read the vocabulary words and check the words they already know.

- Play the audio so students can hear the vocabulary words.

Exercise B. | Meaning from Context
Have students work individually to choose the correct word or phrase in parentheses to complete each sentence.

Answer Key

1. have 2. dance 3. easy 4. words 5. ticket
6. less 7. like 8. in his own way 9. best

track 3-8

Exercise C. | Play the audio. Have students listen and check their answers from exercise **B**.

Exercise D. | Discussion   In small groups, have students discuss the questions about the photographs while recycling target vocabulary words.

Using Vocabulary

Exercise A. | Have students use vocabulary words to complete the conversations individually.

Answer Key

1. song 2. album 3. lively 4. interpret 5. appeal 6. lyrics

track 3-9

Exercise B. | Play the audio as students listen and check their answers in exercise **A**.

Exercise C. | Have students practice the conversations in pairs.

Exercise D.

- Have students read the information and choose the correct words in parentheses.

- Go over the answers as a class.

- Conduct a brief follow-up discussion. For example, have students tell you why the ukulele is popular in Hawaii, or ask them to name another instrument with four strings.

Answer Key

1. appeals 2. afford 3. songs 4. simple 5. perform

TIP   The information about ukulele music is connected to the Lesson B Listening section.

Developing Listening Skills

45 mins

(pages 156-157)

Before Listening

Understanding Visuals | As a preview to the listening passage, have students discuss the photo of musician Jake Shimabukuro in pairs. Tell students to use what they see in the photo as well as the caption to help them answer the questions.

> ### Answer Key *(Answers will vary.)*
>
> Sample Answers:
>
> 1. Based on the photo caption and cues from the photo itself, students may check age (around 30), job (musician), nationality (American, perhaps of Japanese ancestry), other (He enjoys playing the ukulele.)
> 2. His smile tells me he likes playing music.
> 3. Answers will vary.

Listening: A Radio Program

 Exercise A. | Critical Thinking

- Give students time to read the answer choices.
- Play the audio and have students choose the speaker's main purpose.

> ### Answer Key
>
> b. to inform the audience about a musician

 Exercise B. | Note-Taking

- Play the audio a second time.
- Have students listen and fill in the missing information in the partially completed notes.

> ### Answer Key
>
> 1. Peace, Love 2. two 3. a singer 4. play alone

After Listening

Critical Thinking | In small groups, have students discuss the questions, which emphasize expressing opinions and speculating.

 ## Pronunciation: Linking Final Consonants to Vowel Sounds

In the natural flow of speech, speakers often link, or connect, one word to the next. There are several patterns that can be called linking, but a good place to begin is with word-final consonant sounds that connect to word-initial vowel sounds.

- Go over the information in the box.
- Play the audio so students can listen to the examples.

Exercise A. | Have students draw a line to connect the words that are linked. Instruct them to cross out the words that are not linked.

> ### Answer Key
>
> The following words are linked: 1, 4, 5, 6, 7, 8, 10
> Students should cross out: 2, 3, 9

Exercise B. | Have students practice saying the linked pairs of words in exercise **A** with a partner.

 Exercise C. | Have students read and listen to an excerpt from the listening passage that shows consonant-to-vowel linking.

Exercise D. | Have students practice saying the sentences from exercise **C** in pairs.

Pronunciation Note
(Jake) Shimabukuro: sheem-ah-boo-**koo**-row

Exploring Spoken English
(pages 158-159)

30 mins

Grammar: Modals of Necessity

IDEAS FOR...   **Presenting Grammar**

- Write these two sentences on the board: *It's necessary. It's not necessary.*
- Help students generate lists of items under each sentence to illustrate the difference between the two sentences. For example:

  T: Imagine you are going on a trip to Paris in July. You're flying there, and you're staying in a nice hotel. Let's see . . . your passport . . . Is it necessary? (*yes*) OK, and how about your winter jacket? Is it necessary? (*No, not in July.*)

- Tell students the grammar lesson focuses on language that is used for saying what is necessary and what is not necessary.
- Go over the information in the box.

Exercise A. | Have students choose the correct modal expression in parentheses for each sentence.

Answer Key

2. have to 3. must 4. don't need to
5. don't have to 6. must

TIP   Some grammar textbooks often include *must not* alongside *must*. However, *must not* involves prohibition rather than necessity, so it hasn't been included here.

Exercise B.

- Have students work alone to complete each sentence with their own ideas.
- Have partners say their sentences to one another.

TIP   As you go over the information in the Student to Student box, ask students to point out the modals of necessity, which are used for giving reasons when refusing invitations.

track 3-14   **Exercise C.**

- Have students preview the article by looking at the photos and captions.
- Play the audio and have students read along in the Student Book and identify the modals of necessity.

Answer Key

. . . I'm a folk dancer, and I love to perform at special events. To be a folk dancer, you really <u>have to</u> love the culture and the music here. That's the most important thing, but we also <u>need to</u> work hard and practice a lot. We dance in groups, and every person <u>has to</u> know the steps. And you can't buy a traditional dress for folk dancing at the store, so we <u>have to</u> make our own. We wear traditional dresses that only come from this part of Mexico.

Exercise D. | Brainstorming

- Have students compare their answers to exercise **C** in pairs.
- Have partners work together to generate new sentences.

Answer Key *(Answers will vary.)*

Sample Answers:

She needs to be in good health; She has to love music; She must know how to sew; She needs to have enough free time to practice.

Exercise E. | Discussion   Have students share their sentences from exercise **D** in small groups.

Engage: Giving a Group Presentation *(page 160)*

45 mins

WARM-UP

This activity has elements of both role-play and debate, with students making and supporting an argument in favor of art and music education.

- Conduct a brief class discussion about students' experiences with art and music instruction in the past. Ask: *Did you have art classes in school? What did you do in art class? Did you enjoy it?*

- Go over the information at the top of page 160.

Exercise A. | Self-Reflection In small groups, have students reflect on their own experiences with art and music.

Exercise B. | Preparation

- Go over the information in the Situation box.

- Go over the information in the Critical Thinking Focus box.

> **TIP** Make sure your students understand that supporting an argument is an extremely important academic skill. This skill can be applied to an oral presentation such as this one, any kind of academic writing, a class discussion, or other situations when we use reason and logic to make a point.

Exercise C. | Preparing an Argument

Have small groups discuss the questions in the chart and create a list of benefits of art and music education.

> **TIP** Ask groups to divide the list—making sure that different students make lists for each topic. As a result, groups will be able to easily to divide the speaking task when the time comes.

Exercise D. | Planning a Presentation

- Give students time guidelines for their presentation.

- Have students plan their presentations so that every group member has a speaking role.

- Tell students that they can organize their presentations according to the chart on this page or in another way that makes sense to them.

Exercise E. | Presentation Have small groups present their arguments to the class. For this group presentation, you may want to have students sit at a table facing the rest of the class.

> **TIP** Give each group written feedback. Focus on how well the group supported its argument.

Our Relationship with Nature

Academic Track
Natural Science/
Anthropology

Academic Pathways:
Lesson A: Listening to a Lecture
Comparing Three Natural
Attractions
Lesson B: Listening to a Conversation
Giving an Individual Presentation

Unit Theme

With the majority of the world's seven billion people living in cities, it can be easy to forget about the close relationship human beings have with nature.

Unit 9 explores the relationship between people and the natural world in terms of:
– cultures closely associated with animals
– hunting and studying wild animals
– tourism in wild places
– conflict between humans and wildlife
– the importance of the natural world in one's own life

Think and Discuss *(page 161)*

5 mins

The Tambopata National Reserve in southeastern Peru is a complex ecosystem that includes rivers, forests, and many species of plants and animals. Like many places, Peru has a growing human population, but it also understands the value of preserving this part of the Amazon basin for future generations.

- Have students read the title and the Academic Pathways as a brief preview of the unit.

- Discuss the questions.

TIP If you have a world map in the classroom, show students where the Tambopata National Reserve is located.

- Give students time to look at the photos and read the captions themselves, or read the captions aloud to the class and have students read along in the Student Book.

- Discuss the questions.

TIP Before continuing with the rest of the unit, ask students to think about the photos and information on pages 161 to 163 and to write down two or three questions they have about the topics. Have students share these questions in pairs or small groups to inspire each other to take an active approach to the unit content.

Pronunciation Note
Tambopata (Reserve): tam-bow-**pah**-ta

Exploring the Theme: Our Relationship with Nature

15 mins

(pages 162-163)

The opening spread features photographs that illustrate some of the unit content, including a hiker enjoying a spectacular view of nature and fishermen harvesting fish as a source of food and income. In each case, the focus is on ways in which nature affects people and vice versa.

Building and Using Vocabulary *(pages 164-165)*

30 mins

WARM-UP

The Lesson A vocabulary is presented in the context of several short reading passages.

- Ask students to think of animals that are important in their culture.

- List the animals on the board and briefly discuss their importance, for example as food, as pets, as cultural symbols, and so on.

- Tell students they will learn about three cultures that have a close relationship with animals.

Building Vocabulary

Exercise A. | Using a Dictionary
track 3-15

- Have students read the vocabulary words and check the words they already know.

- Play the audio so that students can hear the vocabulary words.

- Give students time to look up unfamiliar words in a dictionary.

Exercise B. | Meaning from Context
track 3-16

- Give students time to read the two passages on page 164 and fill in the blanks.

- Play the audio. Have students read along in the Student Book and check their answers.

- Answer any questions students have about the readings.

Answer Key

1. relationship 2. depend 3. raise 4. share
5. value 6. respect 7. ahead

> **TIP** Tell students that the plural form of *reindeer* is *reindeer*; there is no change in spelling.

> **IDEAS FOR...** Checking Comprehension
>
> To check students' understanding of the readings, ask them questions about the two cultures. For example:
>
> *Which culture lives in Europe: the Sami people or the Maasai people?* (the Sami people)
>
> *Which culture moves to different places with their animals?* (both cultures)

Using Vocabulary

Exercise A. | Self-Reflection In pairs, have students think about and discuss their own culture and the animal or animals associated with it.

> **TIP** Allowing students to reflect on and personalize information does more than just hold their interest. When it comes to cross-cultural communication and other types of relationships, we must first understand our own culture, with its preferences and biases. This makes it possible to understand and accept another person's culture.

Exercise B. | Meaning from Context
track 3-17

- Give students time to read the passage and fill in the blanks.

- Play the audio. Have students read along in the Student Book and check their answers.

> **Answer Key** 1. hunted 2. within 3. responsibility

> **TIP** If students aren't sure about the answers in exercise B, remind them that they'll hear the correct words on the audio.

Exercise C. | Critical Thinking In small groups, have students discuss the questions and recycle target vocabulary.

Developing Listening Skills

45 mins

(pages 166-167)

Before Listening

Exercise A. | Using a Dictionary
This pre-listening exercise presents necessary vocabulary and background information about the topic.

- Give students time to read the passage and look up the underlined words.

- Tell students they will hear more details about the topic in the listening passage.

Exercise B. | Critical Thinking
The grammar points in both Lesson A and B of this unit involve comparisons, so this critical thinking focus provides information about why and how we make comparisons.

- Go over the information in the Critical Thinking Focus box.

- Have students discuss the questions in pairs.

> **Answer Key** *(Answers will vary.)*
>
> 1. The Sami people also live in a cold climate with a lot of snow and ice.
> 2. In both cultures, people hunt (or hunted) animals for food.

Exercise C. | Self-Reflection
Have partners discuss the questions in preparation for the listening passage.

Listening: A Lecture

track 3-18

Exercise A. | Listening for Main Ideas

- Give students time to read the statements.

- Play the audio. Have students decide if each statement is true or false.

> **Answer Key** 1. T 2. F 3. F 4. T

> **TIP** As you go over the answers in exercise A, ask students to recall information from the listening passage that led them to choose *true* or *false*.

track 3-19

Identifying Opinions | Distinguishing between facts and opinions is an important skill, and speakers often use special emphasis when they give opinions.

- Go over the information in the box.

- Play the audio so that students can hear the examples.

track 3-18

Exercise B. | Identifying Opinions

- Give students time to read the questions.

- Play the audio passage a second time. Have students listen and answer the questions.

> **Answer Key** *(Answers may vary.)*
>
> 1. The first student wants to stop seal hunting. He uses negative words such as *difficult* and *awful*. He also uses extra emphasis.
> 2. The third student doesn't think we should kill animals at all. He introduces his opinion with *personally*.

IDEAS FOR... Multi-level Classes

Have students write their answers to the questions in exercise **B** in their notebooks. This gives students of any level time to formulate their answers and be well prepared for the discussion in exercise **C**.

Exercise C. | Discussion
Have students discuss their answers from exercise **B** in pairs.

After Listening

Discussion | Encourage students to express their own opinions as they discuss the topic in small groups.

Exploring Spoken English
(pages 168-170)

45 mins

Grammar: The Comparative and Superlative Forms of Adjectives

IDEAS FOR... Presenting Grammar

- Ask students to look at the photos on page 164. Write *colder* and *larger* on the board. Ask students: *Which people live in a colder climate?* (the Sami people) *Which people herd larger animals?* (the Maasai people)
- Point out that we use words such as *colder* and *larger* to talk about two people or things.
- Write *the most interesting* on the board.
- Point out all three photos in the vocabulary section and ask students: *Which people are the most interesting to you? Why?* Elicit responses from several students.
- Point out that we use phrases such as *the most interesting* to talk about three or more people or things.
- Go over the information in the grammar chart on page 168.

Exercise A. | In pairs, instruct students to use the adjectives in parentheses to make statements with comparative and superlative forms.

Answer Key

2. Fishing is the most dangerous job in my country.
3. Your cookies are more delicious than my cookies.
4. This view is more beautiful than the view from my hotel room.
5. Your apartment is the cleanest apartment in the building.
6. I think cattle are smarter than horses.

TIP If students aren't sure which form to use in exercise A, ask them whether they're talking about two people or things in the statement or more than two.

Exercise B.

- Go over the information in the box at the bottom of page 168.
- Have students fill in the blanks in exercise **B**.
- Instruct partners to practice saying their sentences from exercise **B** to one another.

Answer Key 2. bigger 3. noisier 4. the prettiest 5. worst 6. smaller

Language Function: Making Comparisons

This section provides information about two wildlife studies in order to provide a context for making comparisons.

Exercise A. track 3-20

- Have students preview the article by reading the title and photo captions and looking at the photos.
- Encourage students to predict the article's content by asking them how the two studies are similar and how they are different. (Both studies involve black bears, but only one study involves black bears that are awake.)
- Play the audio and have students read along in the Student Book.

Exercise B. | Collaboration Have partners work together to extract information from the article and make inferences based on logic and prior knowledge.

TIP Go over the directions for both exercises B and C at the same time. That way partners can discuss their ideas as they fill in the Venn diagram.

Exercise C. | Using a Graphic Organizer

Have students work in pairs as they fill in the Venn diagram. Refer students to page 214 of the *Independent Student Handbook* for more information on using Venn diagrams.

TIP Students may not agree on every point about the bear studies, but the goal of the activity is to be able to participate in a discussion about the studies and practice using this type of graphic organizer.

Answer Key *(Answers will vary.)*

New Jersey Study: a bear's health

Both Studies: number of bears in an area; number of cubs each year; a bear's age; a bear's location

Minnesota Study: bears' favorite foods; how mother bears raise cubs; how cubs play together; how bears react to danger; how bears react to other bears

Exercise D. | Critical Thinking
Instruct students to make inferences and draw conclusions about the two bear studies as they practice using the comparative form with a partner.

Exercise E. |
Have students share their ideas from exercise **D** in small groups.

IDEAS FOR... Expansion

- Call on one student from each small group to report on one aspect of their group's discussion. Ask them, for example, to tell the class about an idea they all agreed on or disagreed on, or to explain the reasons for one of their ideas.
- Have students use the Internet to find out one additional interesting fact about each of the two bear studies. Then ask students to share the facts in the next class.

Speaking *(page 171)*

30-45 mins

Comparing Three Natural Attractions

WARM-UP

In this Speaking activity, students work together in pairs to choose a natural attraction they would like to visit.

- If you have a projector in the classroom, show students photos from a visit you made to a beautiful natural area and tell the class about your visit.

- As an alternative, bring to class enough brochures from a natural attraction in your part of the world for students to look at.

- Conduct a brief class discussion about natural attractions students have visited and whether they might enjoy a visit to the place you've shown them in the photos or brochures.

Exercise A. | Self-Reflection

- Go over the directions for item 1 and have students circle their choice.

- Go over the directions for item 2 and have students check the appropriate boxes and add their own ideas.

- Put students into pairs to discuss their answers.

Exercise B.

- Preview the activity by pointing out the three photos, saying the names of the places and asking students whether they have heard about each place.

- Give students time to read about the tour packages.

Pronunciation Note
Iguazú (Falls): ee-gwah-**soo**
Colca (Canyon): **kol**-kah
Galápagos (Islands): ga-**lop**-a-gus

Exercise C.

- Go over the directions. Ask two student volunteers to read the speech bubbles aloud.

- Have partners discuss the tours using the comparative and superlative.

Answer Key *(Answers will vary.)*

Sample Answers:

S1: The scenery at Iguazú Falls is more amazing than the scenery of the Galápagos Islands.

S2: That's true, but the wildlife in the Galápagos Islands is more interesting than the wildlife at Iguazú Falls.

S1: The tour of the Galápagos Islands is the longest tour.

TIP After partners have decided which natural attraction to visit, have them share their choice and the reasons for it with the class or with another pair of students.

Viewing: Horses *(pages 172-173)*

30 mins

Overview of the Video | Domesticated animals have obvious significance in the lives of human beings, and horses—used for transportation, sport, and even milk and meat in some cultures—have played a major role in human history. There is also a special quality in horses that most other domesticated animals just don't have. Perhaps this quality is due to their size and speed, or to the wildness we see in them.

Before Viewing

Exercise A. | Prior Knowledge   Have pairs of students discuss the role that horses have played in the lives of people.

Exercise B. | Using a Dictionary   Have students match each word to its definition, using a dictionary if needed.

> **Answer Key**   1. c 2. a 3. e 4. b 5. d

Exercise C. | Understanding Visuals
This exercise uses the form of a somewhat unusual time line. The events are presented in chronological order, and students must think about the relationships between the events and when they happened in order to extract meaning from the time line.

- Give students time to read the time line.

- Ask a student volunteer to read the example in the speech bubble aloud.

- Have students make statements about the time line in pairs.

> **TIP**   Remind students of the useful time expressions on page 136 of Unit 7.

While Viewing

Exercise A.
3:12

- Give students time to read the statements.

- Play the video without the captions. Have students watch and listen for each of the four topics.

> **Answer Key**   3, 1, 4, 2

> **TIP**   Students will not hear the exact words they read in exercise A. They need to listen for the main ideas.

Exercise B.
3:12

- Play the video again—with or without the captions.

- Instruct students to listen and draw lines from the words for different types of horses to the corresponding illustrations.

> **Answer Key**
>
> From left to right, the pictures show a pony, a racehorse, and a draft horse.

After Viewing

Critical Thinking | Have students discuss the questions in small groups. Encourage them to focus on interpreting the quotation while drawing on prior knowledge.

> **Answer Key** *(Answers will vary.)*
>
> Sample Answers:
>
> 1. The statement means that horses were an important form of transportation for people in the past. Before people began to use horses for transportation, they could only walk or run from place to place. Horses can run faster than people, and they can carry heavy loads or pull a cart or wagon. They can also walk for many hours before they get tired.
>
> 2. walking, running, donkeys, etc.

Building and Using Vocabulary *(pages 174-175)*

30 mins

WARM-UP

The Lesson B vocabulary is presented in the context of conversations about a gorilla-watching tour.

■ Point out the photos of gorillas in this vocabulary section.

■ Ask students a few questions about gorillas. For example: *Are gorillas large or small animals?* (large) *Are gorillas dangerous or not dangerous?* (Answers may vary.) *Do gorillas live in warm climates or cold climates?* (warm)

■ Remind students of the tours of natural attractions they saw on page 171. Tell them that in Uganda, in Africa, people go on tours in order to see gorillas.

Building Vocabulary

Exercise A. | Using a Dictionary
track 3-21

■ Have students read the vocabulary words and check the words they already know.

■ Play the audio so that students can hear the vocabulary words.

■ Give students time to look up unfamiliar words in a dictionary.

Exercise B. | Meaning from Context
track 3-22

■ Have students look at the photos and read the captions.

■ Instruct students to read the conversations and circle the correct words.

■ Play the audio. Have students read along in the Student Book and check their answers.

Answer Key

1. wildlife	5. aggressive	9. save
2. scenery	6. avoid	10. limited
3. is worth	7. conflict	
4. attack	8. reserve	

Exercise C. | Have students practice the conversations from exercise **B** in pairs.

Using Vocabulary

Exercise A. | The sentences in this activity are about gorillas and gorilla tours in Uganda's Bwindi Impenetrable National Park. Have students fill in the blanks with the target vocabulary words.

Answer Key

1. save 2. limited 3. is worth 4. conflict, reserve
5. wildlife, scenery 6. avoid 7. attack 8. aggressive

TIP Encourage students to use context clues, including grammatical function, as they complete exercise A. Ask, for example: *What kind of word do you need here—a noun, a verb, or an adjective?*

Exercise B. | Discussion Have students discuss the questions in small groups, giving them a chance to personalize the topics.

Exercise C. | Critical Thinking Have students discuss the gorilla facts in their small groups. The focus is on finding information that interests or surprises each student in some way.

IDEAS FOR... Expansion

The topic of eco-tourism is relevant in many parts of the world, and it has added an economic incentive to the ethical and biological reasons for environmental conservation.

■ Find a guest speaker to visit your class and talk about the natural attractions in your area. The speaker could be an expert or a person who just enjoys visiting such places.

■ Before the visit, have students think of questions to ask the speaker. Also give the speaker some background information about the class, including the students' interests and language level.

Developing Listening Skills
(pages 176-177)

45 mins

Before Listening

- Point to the photo on page 176. As a scanning exercise, ask students questions with answers that are easy to find in the paragraph. For example: *What is this?* (a dam) *What's the name of the river?* (the Zambezi River)

- Give students time to read the rest of the information in the paragraph.

Listening: A Conversation

track 3-23

Exercise A. | Listening for Main Ideas

- Give students time to read the questions and answer choices.

- Play the audio. Have students choose the correct answer.

Answer Key

c. There are benefits to having animals in and near Kariba Town. However, there are also some conflicts between people and animals there.

track 3-23

Exercise B. | Listening for Details

In this exercise, students check the African animals that are mentioned in the listening.

- Say the name of each animal in the list and have students repeat after you.

- Play the audio. Have students check the animals they hear mentioned.

Answer Key

baboons, elephants, leopards, zebras

After Listening

Discussion | The focus of this activity is on making inferences based on information from the listening passage. Have students discuss the questions in small groups.

IDEAS FOR... Checking Comprehension

After students discuss the questions, go through the questions and call on students at random to tell you their group's answer as well as the reasons for it. Since inferences are based on evidence, students should be able to give you specific details from the listening that led to their answers.

track 3-24

Pronunciation: Using Stress for Emphasis

Emphatic stress is usually easy to hear, but interpreting the reasons for a speaker's extra emphasis requires some thought and practice.

- Go over the information in the box.

- Play the audio so that students can hear the examples.

track 3-25

Exercise A.

- Give students time to read the excerpt from the listening passage.

- Play the audio and have students read along in the Student Book.

Exercise B.

- Have students work in small groups to analyze the emphatic stress from the excerpt in exercise **A**.

- Give students the suggested answers, but stay open to differences of opinion.

- Go over the information in the Student to Student box.

- Ask students whether they remember how the speakers in the listening passage ended their conversation.

Answer Key *(Answers may vary. Suggested answers are below.)*

Shows emotion: really, imagine, house, imagine, easy, baboons, zebras, amazing, that

Emphasizes meaning: old, was

TIP   It's fine to play the audio as many times as necessary depending on your students' needs and the amount of time you have. Although real life usually doesn't allow learners to listen to something multiple times, in-class practice can help students develop their listening skills as well as their confidence.

Exploring Spoken English
(pages 178-179)

30 mins

Grammar: Comparisons with *As . . . As*

> **IDEAS FOR... Presenting Grammar**
>
> - Bring to class two examples of one particular item such as two coffee cups. The items should be exactly the same.
> - Ask students questions about the items using the comparative. For example: *Is this cup larger than the other cup?* (no) *Is this cup more colorful than the other cup?* (no)
> - Tell students they will learn about using *as . . . as* to talk about things that are (or are not) the same.
> - Go over the information in the grammar box.

Exercise A. | Instruct students to use *as . . . as* or *not as . . . as* along with the words in the exercise to give their opinions about pairs of items.

> **Answer Key** *(Answers will vary.)*
>
> 2. Oranges are (not) as delicious as chocolate.
> 3. Chocolate is (not) as nutritious as oranges.
> 4. Black bears are (not) as aggressive as baboons.
> 5. Reindeer are (not) as large as camels.
> 6. Lions are (not) as beautiful as tigers.

Exercise B. | The Penguin Fact File is a graphic that presents information about two penguin species. Have students use the information in the graphic and the adjectives in the box to say as many sentences as they can think of with a partner.

> **Answer Key** *(Answers will vary.)*
>
> Sample Answers:
>
> Adélie penguins are not as colorful as Rockhopper penguins. Rockhopper penguins don't live as long as Adélie penguins. Rockhopper penguins are not as numerous as Adélie penguins. Adélie penguins are as tall as Rockhopper penguins.

> **TIP** Make sure students understand how the information in the Penguin Fact File is presented. Say, for example: *This fact file has information about two penguin species, the Adélie penguin here on the left, and the Rockhopper penguin on the right. Who can tell me how long the Rockhopper penguin usually lives?* (10 years) *Good. That's its lifespan. Are there any questions about the fact file?*

track 3-26

Exercise C.

- Have students preview the article by looking at the photos and reading the title and photo captions.
- Play the audio. Have students listen and read along in the Student Book.

Exercise D. | Critical Thinking Have students work in pairs to decide if each statement is true or false.

> **Answer Key** *(Answers may vary.)*
>
> 1. T 2. T 3. F

> **TIP** Only item 1 in exercise D can be answered with certainty. Partners can discuss the remaining statements and try to agree on an answer.

Exercise E. | Discussion

- Ask the partners from exercise **D** to join another pair of students.
- Have students discuss the questions in small groups.

Engage: Giving an Individual Presentation *(page 180)*

45 mins

WARM-UP

- Go over the information at the top of page 180.

- Conduct a brief review of the presentation skills students have already learned. For example, ask students how they should begin a presentation (introduce themselves); how they can organize their presentation and remember what they want to say (make notes); how they can keep the audience interested (make eye contact, give interesting details); and so on.

- A list of the classroom presentation skills can be found in the Scope and Sequence at the beginning of the Student Book. You may also want to refer students to pages 211–213 of the *Independent Student Handbook* for more information about classroom presentation skills.

> **TIP** Although this Engage activity asks students to give a presentation to the whole class, you may need to modify the activity if time will not permit you to do this. If this is the case, have students give their presentations in small groups. Create and distribute feedback forms so that students can evaluate their group members' presentations.

Exercise A. | Brainstorming Have students begin by brainstorming a list of ideas about ways in which the natural world is important to them.

Exercise B. | Using a Graphic Organizer

- As a class, go over the directions and the list of bullet points.

- Look at the example spider map together and give students an example of a main idea (e.g., animals are helpful to people) and an example of a detail (e.g., farmers use donkeys to carry fruits and vegetables to the market).

- Tell students how much time they will have to give their presentations.

Exercise C. | Planning a Presentation

- As a class, go over the directions and the list of bullet points.

- Go over the information about ending a presentation with a strong conclusion in the Presentation Skills box.

- Students plan their presentations and make notes to use during their presentations.

Exercise D. | Practicing Your Presentation
Have partners practice their presentations and give each other feedback.

> **TIP** Let students know how you will evaluate their presentations. If you have created feedback forms for yourself or for students, show students the evaluation criteria at this time.

Exercise E. | Presentation Have students give their presentations.

> **TIP** Have students stand up behind a table or podium to give their presentations. This arrangement will resemble the kind of setting that students will encounter in future business or educational presentations.

How We Communicate

Academic Track
Interdisciplinary

Academic Pathways:
Lesson A: Listening to a News Report
Talking about the Recent Past
Lesson B: Listening to a Telephone Conversation
Giving a Presentation and
Answering Questions

Unit Theme

Communication has obvious importance in our daily lives. It's also a topic that everyone has experience with but can always learn something new about.

Unit 10 presents the topic of communication as it relates to:

– verbal and non-verbal communication
– using the Internet for communication
– inventions and devices for communication
– communication for blind people
– electronic garbage on Earth and in space

Think and Discuss *(page 181)*

5 mins

The photo shows two Greek men wearing traditional regional clothing. They seem to be engaged in an earnest conversation, and their body language is especially interesting.

- Discuss the questions.

- Encourage students to comment on how the men are sitting, their eye contact (or lack of it) in the moment the picture was taken, and the ways in which these men might communicate in their daily lives. For example, do students think the men send emails or text messages very often?

> **TIP** If students aren't sure how to answer question 3, have them read the Academic Pathways at the top of the page and then flip through the unit in order to preview the topics.

Exploring the Theme: How We Communicate *(pages 182-183)*

15 mins

The opening spread features some of the enclosed satellite dishes that are used for military communications at Menwith Hill in England. The spread also features smaller photos that introduce the unit themes of verbal, non-verbal, and written communication as well as the use of technology for communication.

The photo captions include key vocabulary and concepts.

- Give students time to look at the photos and read the captions.

- Discuss the questions.

- Ask students to look back at the photo on page 181 and tell you what kind or kinds of communication it shows (verbal communication and body language—a kind of non-verbal communication).

> **TIP** The bilingual stop sign in the photo depicting written communication includes both the English and Inuktitut languages. The picture was taken in Nunavut, the largest territory in Canada and home to thousands of Inuit people.

Building and Using Vocabulary *(pages 184-185)*

30 mins

WARM-UP

To recycle some of the terms and concepts from the opening spread and preview the vocabulary section, ask students: *What kinds of communication do you see in the photos on pages 184 and 185?* Students might mention email or the Internet, texting, talking, and non-verbal communication. Even the man in the last photo appears to be smiling slightly and making eye contact with the photographer—both of which are kinds of non-verbal communication.

Building Vocabulary

track 3-27

Exercise A. | Using a Dictionary

- Have students read the vocabulary words and check the words they already know.

- Play the audio so that students can hear the vocabulary words.

- Give students time to look up unfamiliar words in a dictionary.

Exercise B. | Have students write each vocabulary word next to the correct definition.

Answer Key

1. involved	5. device	9. access
2. speed	6. message	10. unfortunately
3. connect	7. basic	
4. represent	8. contact	

> **TIP** Since the definitions in students' dictionaries are probably somewhat different from the definitions in exercise B, the activity goes beyond matching and encourages students to think about each word's meaning.

Exercise C. | Meaning from Context
track 3-28

- Give students time to read the statements and choose the correct words.

- Play the audio and have students check their answers.

Answer Key

1. basic	5. unfortunately	9. represents
2. contact	6. involved	10. speed
3. device	7. connect	
4. access	8. message	

Using Vocabulary

Exercise A. | Give students time to read the information under the photos. Have students discuss the questions in pairs.

Answer Key *(Answers will vary.)*

1. I usually <u>contact</u> my friends and family by telephone or by email.

2. Turtles move at a low <u>speed</u>, and trains move at a high <u>speed</u>.

3. The <u>basic</u> parts of a presentation are the introduction, body, and conclusion. You need to include your main ideas and some interesting details.

4. a. number b. and c. plus d. percent e. exclamation

5. I'm <u>involved</u> in a reading group because I enjoy discussing books.

Exercise B. | Meaning from Context   Instruct students to fill in the blanks with words from the box.

Answer Key   1. access 2. message 3. device 4. connect

> **TIP** The article in exercise B serves as background information for the Lesson A listening passage.

IDEAS FOR...   Checking Comprehension

Since the importance of Ken Banks's invention may be difficult to grasp in an age of widespread Internet access, conduct a brief class discussion about the article in exercise **B**. Ask: *Can you think of some places where it's difficult to access the Internet?* (e.g., rural areas, poorer countries, etc.) *In those places, do you think people have very expensive telephones or very basic telephones?* (very basic)

Developing Listening Skills

(pages 186-187)

track 3-29

Pronunciation: Thought Groups

Thought groups are an important part of the rhythm and intonation of English. Although it is difficult to provide exact guidelines for their use, raising students' awareness of thought groups can improve their listening comprehension as well as their own intelligibility when speaking.

- Go over the information in the box.
- Play the audio so that students can hear the examples.

track 3-30

Exercise A.

- Give students time to read the text.
- Play the audio and have students read along in the Student Book.

> **TIP** Students at this level may not have the grammatical knowledge to notice that thought groups often consist of a grammatical unit such as a clause, a verb phrase, a prepositional phrase, and so on. Referring to thought groups as "one idea" may be helpful, however.

track 3-31

Exercise B.

- Play the audio and have students read along in the Student Book.
- Have partners practice saying the sentences.

> **TIP** As students practice saying the sentences, encourage them to say each thought group smoothly—connecting the individual words into one idea.

Before Listening

Have students prepare for and personalize the listening topic by considering the difficulties of life without access to the Internet.

Listening: A News Report

track 3-32

Exercise A. | Listening for Main Ideas

- Give students time to read the statements and answer choices.
- Play the audio. Have students listen and choose the correct answers.

Answer Key   1. b 2. b 3. c

Exercise B. | Making Inferences
track 3-32

- Give students time to read the statements.
- Play the audio. Have students listen and decide if each statement is true or false.

Answer Key   1. F 2. T 3. F 4. T

After Listening

Exercise A. | Critical Thinking   Have pairs of students discuss the questions.

Exercise B. | Have partners discuss their answers from exercise **A** with another pair of students.

> **IDEAS FOR...   Expansion**
>
> National Geographic's Emerging Explorers Program supports young scientists, inventors such as Ken Banks, adventurers, and even a few singers and storytellers. For homework, direct students to information about the program at the National Geographic Web site. Have students read about and take brief notes on one emerging explorer who interests them. Then in class, have students form small groups and tell classmates about the explorer they chose.

Exploring Spoken English
(pages 188-190)

45 mins

Grammar: The Present Perfect Tense

IDEAS FOR... Presenting Grammar

- Write two sentences using the present perfect on the board. Ask students to choose the correct word: *have* or *has*.

   1. My parents (<u>have</u> / has) lived in Belarus for 30 years. (*have*)

   2. Lorena (have / <u>has</u>) always enjoyed dancing. (*has*)

- Point out to students that the present perfect verb tense is used in these sentences.

- Ask students when or why we use the present perfect. (*Answers will vary. The point is to get students to think about the verb tense.*)

- Go over the information in the grammar box. Make sure partners say complete sentences using the present perfect tense.

Answer Key *(Answers may vary.)*

2. Celine hasn't visited her family in Romania since 2009.

3. Randal has cooked a delicious meal. Can you join us for dinner?

4. I haven't seen the new action movie. Let's go see it tonight!

5. He has called me twice today.

6. They've known each other a long time.

> **TIP** After students complete the grammar exercise, call on a different student to say each sentence to the class.

Language Function

Talking about Duration: The Present Perfect Tense with *For* and *Since* | This information helps students determine when to use *for* and when to use *since* with the present perfect.

 Exercise A.
track 3-33

- Give students time to fill in the blanks in the conversation.

- Play the audio. Have students check their answers

Answer Key 1. since 2. for 3. for 4. since

Exercise B. | Have students practice the conversation from exercise **A** in pairs.

Exercise C. | **Collaboration** Have students work together to plot the events, which are not listed in chronological order, on the time line.

> **TIP** Exercise C provides students with information they need for exercise D.

Exercise D. | Ask students to work individually or in pairs to fill in the blanks in the conversations.

Answer Key

1. 1829 2. existed 3. around 140 years 4. since 5. 1979

Note: The answer to item 3 will vary based on the current year.

Exercise E. | Have partners practice the conversations from exercise **D**.

Exercise F. | Have students use the conversations from exercise **D** as models to create their own exchanges about the events from the time line on page 189.

IDEAS FOR... Multi-level Classes

For exercises **C** through **F**, students can work at their own pace. If higher-level students finish an activity early, tell them to go on to the next exercise. Then when partners reach exercise **F**, which is relatively uncontrolled, they can create more or fewer new statements depending on the remaining time.

Exercise G. | Discussion Have students discuss the questions in small groups. The focus is on reflecting on one's own communication habits.

> **TIP** If class time allows, call on different students to report on their own or their group's answers to the discussion questions from exercise **G**. This will provide a low-stress opportunity for students to address the whole class.

Speaking *(page 191)*

30-45 mins

Talking about the Recent Past

Exercise A. | Have students work individually to match the questions and answers.

Answer Key 1. b 2. d 3. e 4. a 5. f 6. c

> **TIP** Originally, the word *theater* only referred to a place where live dramas were performed by actors on a stage. In American English, however, *theater* or *movie theater* may also refer to a cinema where films or movies are shown.

Exercise B. | Have students practice saying the questions and answers from exercise **A** in pairs.

> **TIP** Encourage students to ask questions about any answers they disagree on.

track 3-34 **Exercise C.**

- Play the audio and have students read along in the Student Book.

- Have students practice the conversation in pairs.

- Ask students to identify the verb tenses the speakers use. Write the following sentences from the conversation on the board and ask students to supply answers.

  - Have you written a letter . . . ?
    Have you used a videophone . . . ? *(present perfect)*

  - I wrote a letter . . .
    I talked with my brother . . . *(simple past)*

  - Yes, my grandma doesn't use email.
    Oh, I see. *(simple present)*

Exercise D. | Have students work individually to add to the list of ideas and language to use in exercise **E**.

> **IDEAS FOR...** **Expansion**
> Create a class list of students' ideas from exercise **D** on the board. This will provide even more language and content that partners can use in their free conversations in exercise **E**.

Exercise E. | Encourage partners to have their own conversations about the topic using the list from exercise **D** and their own ideas, with the conversation from exercise **C** serving as a model.

Viewing: Touching the Stars
(pages 192-193)

30 mins

Overview of the Video | Many forms of communication, from reading words on a page to listening to a lecture or a friend's voice, depend on the senses of sight and sound. Yet people with impaired vision or hearing also need to communicate.

This video shows a special collaboration between NASA (the National Aeronautics and Space Administration) and visually-impaired students at a school for the blind in the USA as they make improvements to an early version of a book about the Hubble Space Telescope.

Before Viewing

Exercise A. | Critical Thinking Have students discuss the questions in small groups. The focus is on considering the communication challenges of deaf and blind people.

 Exercise B. | Using the Present Perfect Tense

track 3-35

■ Give students time to read the paragraph and fill in the blanks.

■ Play the audio. Have students listen and check their answers.

Answer Key

2. have enjoyed **3.** has sent **4.** has had
5. has created (or have created)

While Viewing

 Exercise A.

3:31

■ Give students time to read the statements.

■ Play the video. Have students watch and circle the correct words.

Answer Key

1. have different levels of vision loss
2. change **3.** plastic

IDEAS FOR...   Checking Comprehension

Play the video the first time with only the audio on, or have students close their eyes or face away from the TV screen while viewing. This will help students listen rather than rely on their eyes for information.

Exercise B.

3:31

■ Give students time to read the statements.

■ Play the video. Have students watch and match the questions and answers.

Answer Key   1. c 2. d 3. e 4. a 5. b

TIP   Exercise B presents some of the more difficult terms and important concepts from the video. It is meant to provide language support and to increase (rather than test) students' comprehension.

After Viewing

Critical Thinking | Have students discuss the questions in small groups. The focus is on imagining or sharing prior knowledge of the lives of people who are blind and/or deaf.

TIP   Reinforce the vocabulary by reminding students of the blind caracal they read about on page 179 of Unit 9.

Building and Using Vocabulary *(pages 194-195)*

30 mins

WARM-UP

Much of Lesson B is about garbage—electronic devices that we no longer need as well as larger garbage in space.

- Ask students about their old computers, cell phones, and other communication devices. What do they do with those items when they no longer need them or want them?

Building Vocabulary

track 3-36

Exercise A. | Meaning from Context

The Lesson B vocabulary is presented in the context of an article about the problem of aging communications satellites.

- Have students preview the article by looking at the illustration and reading the title and the caption.

- Play the audio and have students read along in the Student Book.

Exercise B. | Have students use context clues from the article to match the vocabulary words to the definitions.

Answer Key

1. collision	5. realized	9. prevent
2. garbage	6. sensible	10. reduce
3. response	7. get rid of	
4. metal	8. probable	

TIP   As you go over the answers in exercise B, ask students which context clues from the article helped them to understand each word's meaning. In some cases, students may need the help of a dictionary.

Using Vocabulary

Exercise A. | Using a Dictionary   One of the useful features of any good dictionary is information about the grammatical function of words. The focus in this activity is on word families and passive vocabulary recognition. Students are not asked to actively use these forms of the vocabulary words.

- Point out the parts of speech of the words in exercise **B**, for example, noun or verb.

- Explain that dictionaries give helpful information about a word's part of speech, or its grammatical function in a sentence.

- Point out the example answer *prevention* in the chart. Have students look up *prevent* in their dictionaries. They may find the noun form *prevention* in the same dictionary entry or in a nearby entry.

- Have students complete the chart, using their dictionaries.

- Encourage students to read page 209 of the *Independent Student Handbook* for more information on dictionary skills.

Answer Key

Missing words are: collide (v.), metallic (adj.), prevention (n.), preventive / preventative (adj.), probability (n.), probably (adv.), respond (v.), responsive (adj.), realization (n.)

Exercise B. | Instruct students to use the target vocabulary in the context of sentences by filling in the blanks.

Answer Key

1. reduce 2. prevent 3. sensible
4. probable 5. realize 6. response

Exercise C. | Discussion   Have students discuss the questions in pairs.

Developing Listening Skills

45 mins

(pages 196-197)

Before Listening

Discussion | To prepare for the listening passage, have students discuss the questions, which also recycle some of the Lesson B vocabulary.

Listening: A Telephone Conversation

- Go over the information about telephone conversations in the Student to Student box.

- Ask students if they know some other expressions to use on the telephone. For example: *Is (person's name) there?* or *Can I take a message?*

track 3-37

Exercise A. | Note-Taking

- Give students time to read the questions.

- Play the audio. Have students listen and write short answers.

> **Answer Key** *(Answers may vary.)*
>
> 1. Another plane crossed in front of Todd's plane on the runway. It was scary.
>
> 2. He saw a commercial (TV advertisement) about recycling electronic devices from the comedy network.
>
> 3. The Web site has information about where to recycle old electronic devices and also information about companies that will take their old products back for recycling.

track 3-37

Exercise B. | Listening for Details

- Give students time to read the questions and answer choices.

- Play the audio. Have students listen and choose the correct answers.

> **Answer Key** 1. c 2. b 3. b 4. a

After Listening

Critical Thinking Focus: Drawing Conclusions

Go over the information in the box.

> **TIP** Drawing conclusions is an advanced critical thinking skill that requires practice. It involves recalling prior knowledge, understanding new information, and making inferences based on logic.

track 3-38

Exercise A. | Preparation Play the audio. Have students listen and read along in the Student Book.

Exercise B. | Critical Thinking Have students use information from the article, their prior knowledge, and their ability to make logical inferences as they discuss the questions and draw conclusions about the topic in small groups.

> **Answer Key** *(Answers will vary.)*
>
> 1.
> - Electronic garbage comes from consumers all over the world when they want to get rid of their old electronic devices.
> - It might go to a landfill or a recycling operation.
> - It can cost money to collect, transport, and process old electronics, and there are environmental costs as well.
> - Dangerous chemicals go into the air or the ground.
>
> 2.
> - If electronic garbage comes from consumers in wealthy countries, then they (along with the manufacturers that made the devices and the stores that sell them) are responsible for dealing with the garbage.
> - Even though the high-tech recycling plant requires money, it's worth it since it prevents pollution from dangerous chemicals.

30 mins

Exploring Spoken English
(pages 198-199)

Grammar: The Present Perfect Tense with *Ever, Already,* and *Yet*

> **IDEAS FOR... Presenting Grammar**
>
> - Before class, prepare some questions specifically for the students in your class.
> - As you go over the grammar box, add the questions you prepared to the examples in the chart; for example: *Steven, have you ever taken the TOEFL test? How was it? Laura, have you already finished exercise A? You're fast! Tessa, have we had a quiz on this unit yet?*

Exercise A. | Collaboration

- Have students work individually to choose the correct signal words to complete the conversations.
- Have students practice the conversations in pairs.

Answer Key 1. yet 2. yet 3. ever 4. already 5. yet 6. ever

Exercise B.

- Have students work individually to read and complete the conversation.
- Have students compare answers and practice the conversation in pairs.

Answer Key 1. yet/already 2. yet 3. ever 4. already 5. ever

TIP Tell students that item 1 in exercise B could have more than one correct answer. Most speakers would use the word *yet* to ask about something we expect to have happened—calling an airline when they've lost luggage. On the other hand, *already* might be used to emphasize the idea of "before now."

Exercise C.

- Go over the directions and the speech bubbles as a class.
- In small groups, have students create a to-do list of all the things they think everyone should do in their lifetime if possible.
- Have each group's secretary write the actual list using large, legible handwriting.
- Instruct students to take turns asking each other about the items from their list.

> **IDEAS FOR... Expansion**
>
> Have students write their names on their group's list of ideas. Then collect the lists. If class time allows, choose a few ideas from the lists to ask several students in the class questions starting with "Have you ever . . . ?" Take the lists home and write a comment or two on each list to show your interest. When you return the lists in the next class, students will appreciate your taking the time to read and enjoy their work.

Exercise D. | Critical Thinking

- Go over the directions and the speech bubbles as a class.
- In small groups, have students use the present perfect to speculate about what has happened to the person in each picture.
- As students talk, circulate and offer suggestions. Don't worry if students use other tenses that are also correct, but encourage them to use the present perfect.

Engage: Giving a Presentation and Answering Questions *(page 200)*

45 mins

WARM-UP

In the Unit 9 Engage activity, students learned about ending a presentation with a strong conclusion. In this activity, students find out what to do after they have given their conclusion.

- Ask students how speakers can give a strong conclusion at the end of a presentation. If they don't remember, review the Presentation Skills box on page 180 of Unit 9.

- Go over the introductory information at the top of page 200 so that students know they will be inviting questions from the audience at the end of this presentation.

- Ask students: *What if an audience member asks you a question, but you've already answered the question in your presentation? What should you say?* (Answers will vary.)

- Ask students: *What if an audience member asks you a question, and you don't know the answer? What should you say?* (Answers will vary.)

Presentation Skills

- Go over the three sections of the Presentation Skills box as a class.

- Ask students whether they have experienced any of these situations after doing or listening to a presentation.

TIP Go over the directions for both exercises A and B at the same time. That way, students will understand the presentation assignment before they're asked to choose a topic.

Exercise A. | In small groups, have students choose a presentation topic from the box.

TIP If students think of a different form of communication to talk about, the topic might be fine as long as they can discuss the various aspects of it that are outlined in exercise B.

Exercise B. | Planning a Presentation In small groups, have students plan and practice their presentation by following the four steps.

TIP While students are planning which part of the presentation each group member will do, remind them that everyone should do part of the speaking, and that someone will need to invite questions from the audience at the end of the presentation.

Exercise C. | Presentation Have students give their presentations and conduct question-and-answer sessions.

TIP Give students time limits for their presentations and question-and-answer sessions. Then keep track of the time during the presentations.

CD 1

Unit 1: Living for Work
Lesson A
Building Vocabulary

Track 2   A. Using a Dictionary   Page 4

travel	skills
opportunity	dangerous
experiences	

Track 3   B. Meaning from Context   Page 4

Beverly and Dereck Joubert

Beverly Joubert and her husband Dereck are creative people. Together, they write and make interesting films about animals in Africa. They love to explore different parts of Africa, and the result is 22 films, 10 books, and many articles!

In order to work together, the Jouberts need to communicate well and understand one another. Their films win many awards, but for the Jouberts, making films is an adventure. It is also a way to do something good for endangered animals. They started the *Big Cats Initiative* fund. With this money, the Jouberts can help the lions and other animals they love. Says Dereck, "If there was ever a time to take action, it is now."

Using Vocabulary

Track 4   B.   Page 5

Photographer Annie Griffiths

Annie Griffiths is famous for her beautiful photographs. The photos come from countries all over the world, so it's just a normal part of life for Griffiths to travel.

Living in other countries is not for everyone, but for Griffiths and her children, it's an adventure. Her children especially love the Middle East, and their experiences in that part of the world helped them to learn about other cultures.

Griffiths's work can also be dangerous. Traveling is not always safe. In the Galápagos Islands, Griffiths found herself in the water with sharks one day!

Besides writing and taking pictures, Griffiths teaches photography skills to people who want to become photographers. They know they are learning from one of the best photographers in the world.

Developing Listening Skills

Listening: An Interview

Track 5   A. Listening for Main Ideas   Page 6

Radio Host: Welcome back, listeners. This is Talk Radio 97, and I'm your host, Ray Bellows. Today, we have the opportunity to talk with Annie Griffiths. She's a photographer for the National Geographic Society, and she travels the world to places such as Africa, Australia, the Middle East, and North and South America. Sometimes her work takes her to dangerous places such as on top of mountains, under the water, or in jungles. But she says her experiences in places where there is a war are more frightening than any wild animals or faraway places. Welcome to the show, Annie.

Annie Griffiths: Thank you, Ray. I'm glad to be here.

Radio Host: Now, you travel a lot. What's your favorite part of the world?

Annie Griffiths: Well, I love southern Africa. I like the energy of the people and the wildlife. I also love the Galápagos Islands and Mexico. You know actually, I like so many places that it's hard to choose a favorite!

Radio Host: I can understand that! And why do you like to travel and explore the world so much?

Annie Griffiths: I love to travel because it allows me to learn about different cultures and, you know, different views of the world. I spend most of my time with ordinary people, and I get to experience how people in different places live their lives. I also love taking pictures of wildlife and landscapes.

Radio Host: Well, your job really is an adventure! My job keeps me sitting in this room day after day. Now, I know that you've traveled with your children. Why did you take them with you?

Annie Griffiths: I took my children along on my travels for many reasons. My assignments were often two or three months long, and I couldn't bear to be away from them for so long. Also, I wanted them to be able to see the world themselves. They have become great travelers and have a great perspective now on the world.

Radio Host: What was their favorite place?

Annie Griffiths: My children loved the Middle East. They had so much fun being part of the Bedouin community there. They rode camels and donkeys and learned to milk goats. They also loved Australia because they got to go to the beach almost every day.

Radio Host: Those do sound like wonderful experiences! But how do you communicate with people in so many places? Say, if you don't speak the language, for example. How do you make friends?

Annie Griffiths: I think the key is to get over my own shyness. I start, you know, by smiling and talking to people. Even if I don't know the local language, I will gesture and smile and be a little silly, so that people feel more relaxed around me.

Radio Host: And that helps you to get your amazing pictures, I'm sure! So, what advice do you have for someone who wants to become a photographer? Do they need any special skills?

Annie Griffiths: I actually think that the most important thing a photographer needs is curiosity. You've got to wake up every morning wanting to experience something new, or learn more about something familiar. It's also important to love being creative and to enjoy seeing things in new ways.

Radio Host: That makes sense, and . . . listeners? Does that sound like you? OK, one last question: what's your favorite photo, and what's the story behind it?

Annie Griffiths: My favorite photo is of a man standing on top of Victoria Falls in Zambia. The light is so beautiful. It brings back memories of an unforgettable day at one of the most amazing places on Earth.

Radio Host: That *is* a beautiful picture—one of my favorites, too. Well, that's all the time we have. Thanks very much for being here today, Annie.

Annie Griffiths: No problem. Nice talking to you, Ray.

Exploring Spoken English

Language Function: Communicating that You Don't Understand

Track 6   A.   Page 8

A: I took a job aptitude test today.
B: A job aptitude test? What's that?
A: Well, it's a test of your skills and interests.
B: I see. And did you get the job?
A: I'm not sure what you mean.
B: I mean—you took a job test, right? Did you do well on the test and get the job?
A: Oh, no. The test only shows which job might be good for you.
B: Ah, I see. It helps you to choose the right job.
A: Exactly!

Lesson B

Building Vocabulary

Track 7   A. Meaning from Context   Page 14

Q: What kind of people make good nurses?
A: Well, you have to be organized. For example, I'm in charge of my patients' medicine. I have to give them the correct medicine, so I write everything down in a chart. I get the medicine. Then, I check on my chart that it's the correct one. Nobody gets the wrong medicine that way.
Q: You are well organized!
A: Thanks. It has a big effect on my patients' health, so it's important to me. Nurses also have to be fit because the work is very physical.
Q: What kind of physical work do you do?
A: I stand or walk all the time, and sometimes I have to lift patients up from their beds.

Q: Is teaching a difficult job?
A: Sometimes it is. Although the students are wonderful, the school has a rule I don't like.
Q: What kind of rule?
A: Well, I teach math and science, and I think they're very important subjects. But students here don't have to take both subjects. They can take one or the other and still graduate.
Q: Do you mean they can finish school and never take math, for example?
A: Yes, they can. It's not a good idea, in my opinion.

Q: What does an engineer do every day?
A: Well, there are many kinds of engineers. I'm an industrial engineer. I look at our processes here at the factory, and I search for any problems.
Q: What do you do if you find a problem?
A: I give a presentation to my managers. We have a meeting, and I explain the problem to them. We try to find ways to solve it.
Q: What happens next?
A: They usually follow my suggestions.
Q: So the managers here have a lot of respect for you.
A: Yes, I believe they do respect me. It's one of the reasons I like my job.

Developing Listening Skills

Track 8   Pronunciation: Syllable Stress   Page 16

Examples:
book
doctor
company

Track 9   A.   Page 16

1. nurse
2. study
3. travel
4. remember
5. reporter
6. creative
7. receive
8. skills

Track 10   B.   Page 16

One-syllable Words
cook
fly
know

Two-syllable Words
money
teacher
travel

Three-syllable Words
adventure
amazing
officer
yesterday

Track 11   Before Listening   Page 16

billion   marine biologist   ocean   pollution   tuna

Listening: An Informal Conversation

Track 12   A.   Page 17

Franco: Hi, Becca! I didn't see you in class on Thursday. Where were you?
Becca: Hey, Franco. Yeah, I was sick on Thursday, so I stayed home.
Franco: That's too bad. Do you feel better now?
Becca: I do . . . thanks. So, was it a good class on Thursday?
Franco: Oh, it was great! There was a special presentation by Dr. Sylvia Earle.
Becca: A presentation?
Franco: Yeah. Dr. Earle talked about her career.
Becca: Really? What does she do?
Franco: Well, she's a marine biologist, so . . . I mean—she's in charge of several groups that study the oceans and take care of them.

Track 13   B. Listening for Main Ideas   Page 17

Franco: Hi, Becca! I didn't see you in class on Thursday. Where were you?
Becca: Hey, Franco. Yeah, I was sick on Thursday, so I stayed home.
Franco: That's too bad. Do you feel better now?
Becca: I do . . . thanks. So, was it a good class on Thursday?
Franco: Oh, it was great! There was a special presentation by Dr. Sylvia Earle.
Becca: A presentation?

Franco: Yeah. Dr. Earle talked about her career.

Becca: Really? What does she do?

Franco: Well, she's a marine biologist, so . . . I mean—she's in charge of several groups that study the oceans and take care of them.

Becca: Where did Dr. Earle go to school?

Franco: She graduated from Duke University with a PhD.

Becca: That's a good school. So they study the oceans . . . like—all of the oceans?

Franco: Sure, well, she talked about fish and other life in the oceans. That's what marine biologists study, you know. And she told us that there are almost seven billion people on Earth now.

Becca: Wow! That's a lot of people!

Franco: Right, so all these people are having a big effect on the world's oceans.

Becca: What kind of effect?

Franco: Think about it—a hundred years ago, there were only two billion people on Earth. So all kinds of changes . . . OK, how often do you eat tuna . . . or other fish?

Becca: Not very often. I probably eat fish once or twice a week.

Franco: OK, but here's what Dr. Earle said. . . . Although *you* might not eat a lot of fish, seven billion people eat a lot of fish! And think about the pollution . . . the oceans are getting dirtier.

Becca: I see what you mean. It's sad, really.

Franco: It is sad, but Dr. Earle believes that we—you and I—can help.

Becca: So, what can we do?

Franco: She said we could stop eating tuna and other large fish, for example.

Becca: Yeah, that's no problem for me. Did Dr. Earle say anything else?

Franco: A lot of things. . . . Oh! She also showed us some beautiful pictures! She swims in the ocean all the time, and she searches for fish or other kinds of sea life . . .

Becca: She must be in good physical health.

Franco: I guess so. Anyway, she looked really healthy, and the presentation was well organized and really interesting!

Engage: Giving a Short Presentation about Yourself

Track 14   B.   Page 20

Hi, everyone. My name is Alejandro, but please call me Alex. I'm from Bogotá. As you know, that's the capital city of Colombia. I'm studying English now, and I'm also studying international relations. In my free time, I like to play tennis or send text messages to my friends. One interesting fact about me is that I have a pretty large family. I live with my parents, two sisters and one brother, and two grandparents as well.

Unit 2: Good Times, Good Feelings
Lesson A

Building Vocabulary

Track 15   A.   Page 24

funny
joke
joy
laughter

led
noise
recorded
researchers
situations
unique

Track 16   B. Meaning from Context   Page 24

From Pant-Pant to Ha-Ha

Look at the photo. Does this look like laughter? New research says that apes laugh when they are tickled. Researchers at the University of Portsmouth led a "tickle team." The group of researchers tickled the necks, feet, hands, and armpits of young apes. The team recorded more than 800 of the resulting laughs on tape. The research suggests that the apes' panting noise is the sound of laughter. They think that this panting is the basis for human expressions of joy—the "ha-ha" sound we make when we laugh. When we find something funny, such as a joke, we laugh. When apes find something funny, such as a tickle, they laugh. Humans find many situations funny—such as jokes, tickles, TV comedy shows—but we are not unique because animals laugh, too.

Developing Listening Skills

Listening: A Lecture

Track 17   A. Understanding the Speaker's Purpose   Page 26

OK, well . . . today we're starting a new topic. . . . It's a fun topic, but it's also serious science. We're looking at laughter—laughter in both human beings and in animals. Of course, human beings know how to laugh, even as babies. We laugh, we laugh before we can talk. But human beings are not unique when it comes to laughter. So . . . let's start with animals. Do apes laugh? How about, how about rats? Do rats laugh? Funnily enough, yes they do.

Track 18   B. Checking Predictions   Page 27

OK, well . . . today we're starting a new topic. . . . It's a fun topic, but it's also serious science. We're looking at laughter—laughter in both human beings and in animals. Of course, human beings know how to laugh, even as babies. We laugh, we laugh before we can talk. But human beings are not unique when it comes to laughter. So . . . let's start with animals. Do apes laugh? How about, how about rats? Do rats laugh? Funnily enough, yes they do.

Ah . . . now we're all laughing. That's because we usually laugh when we hear other people laugh. But we'll get to that in a minute. First, let's answer the question: Why do animals laugh? Well, one researcher at Bowling Green State University studies rats. He, he noticed that young rats—like many young animals—like to play. And animals like to play because it's fun. It feels good to them. So Professor Panksepp—from Bowling Green University—began to tickle the rats. . . . Really! You can find videos of it online! OK, and what did he hear? Well he heard nothing at first. The rats' laughter was at a very high frequency—too high for human ears to hear it. But with special equipment he was able to hear noises from the rats when he tickled them. The rats were having fun, and they liked to be tickled! According to the professor, the rats' laughter is a way to communicate. It's a sound of joy, and it, it tells other rats, "Hey! This is fun! Let's play some more!"

Apes are another animal that like tickling. Tickling leads them to a sort of, a kind of panting sound. Researchers in the UK recorded a lot of apes making this sound, and they think it's a form of laughter. Early humans probably made a similar sound, but over time, that sound became the "ha ha" sound we know as laughter today.

So, that brings us to human beings like you and me. We all, all of us understand laughter, and all of us—no matter what language we speak—laugh in the same way, more or less. Doctor Robert Provine studies human laughter, and he, he noticed some interesting things about it. First, do jokes make you laugh? Do funny stories make you laugh? Maybe they do. But most laughter—more than 80 percent of it—does not happen because of a joke. Provine says that human beings—that people laugh in social situations. They laugh at something their friend says, or they laugh at something they see, but again—something they see with their friends. People don't usually laugh alone.

Provine also studies TV shows—comedy shows on television. One thing TV producers know—if one person laughs, other people start to laugh. So these shows, these TV shows have a laugh track—you know, you're watching the show, and you can hear the audience laughing. Believe it or not, the show doesn't even have a real audience! They use recorded laughter to make . . .

Track 19 Pronunciation: The Intonation of *Yes/No* Questions Page 30

Examples:
Do you think it is funny?
Is she really laughing?

Track 20 A. Page 30

1. **A:** Do you laugh a lot?
   B: Yes, I do.
2. **A:** Do you like weddings?
   B: I love weddings.
3. **A:** Do you like sitcoms?
   B: Some of them are OK.
4. **A:** Do you go to many parties?
   B: No, not really.

Lesson B
Building Vocabulary

Track 21 A. Meaning from Context Page 34

I don't have much free time because I have a full-time job. I also have children, so I like to spend time with them. Sometimes we go to the beach, and sometimes we go to the park. For me, playing with my children has some important benefits: It makes me feel young and gives me great joy.

I enjoy taking walks in the park. I love the outdoors—seeing the trees and feeling the sun on my face. Basically, I'm always moving. Walking is good exercise. All that exercise keeps me healthy.

What do I do in my free time? Well, my hobby is cooking. It's a pretty common hobby, so I know a lot of other people who like to cook. Sometimes my friends come over and we cook together. We laugh and tell stories!

When I want to relax, I listen to music at home. My favorite music is classical, especially Mozart. There's only one drawback to spending my free time at home: I almost never spend time outside.

Developing Listening Skills
Listening: A Talk with Questions and Answers

Track 22 A. Listening for Main Ideas Page 36

Instructor: OK, now, let's welcome our guest speaker Mark Johnson. Mark, Mark works for the city government. He manages the parks department.
Guest Speaker: Thanks. Thanks a lot. Yes, hello, I'm Mark Johnson. It's nice to meet you all. I wanted to talk to you about some of the benefits of parks. First, I have a question for you, though. Who goes to River Park?
Student 1: I do. I walk through the park every day.
Student 2: I, um, I sometimes go there on the weekends. In fact, last Sunday, there was a really good concert there.
Guest Speaker: Good, good—so I know you enjoy the parks, and you get some benefits from going there. I want to, I'd like to go into more detail now and talk about our research. First, one of the most common reasons people go to parks is for exercise. Yes?
Student 2: Yes, that surprises me a little. What kind of exercise?
Guest Speaker: Actually, the most important type of exercise for most people is walking. Recently, research in the Netherlands and Japan found that people who live near parks—in other words, people who had good places to walk—were healthier than other people.
Student 3: That's interesting! Why is it healthier?
Guest Speaker: Well, diabetes and high blood pressure were less common among people who walked, and they were less likely to be overweight. And besides, besides the health benefits, parks provide social benefits as well. A recent study in Chicago showed that crime falls when there are more green spaces. The study looked at 98 apartment buildings and found that crime was 50 percent lower around buildings that had lots of trees and green spaces.
Student 1: That all sounds great, but what are the drawbacks?
Guest Speaker: I'm sorry? I, I missed that.
Student 1: OK, I'll speak up. . . . I said, what are the drawbacks?
Guest Speaker: That's a good question, and in fact, parks cost money. Cities have to buy land, and build walkways and play areas; and they have to pay people to take care of the parks. But here's the, here's the thing: We know now that having nice places where people can spend their free time is very important. Healthy, happy people have fewer problems, so cities don't have to spend as much money on things such as police and medical care.
Instructor: That's an important point, and I think there might be some questions. Anyone? Yes . . . Karen?

Track 23 Pronunciation: The Intonation of *Wh-* Questions   Page 37

Examples:
Where is the nearest park?
When are you going?

Track 24   A.   Page 37

Conversation 1:
Candice: What's the name of the park?
Alexis: It's called the High Line.
Candice: Where is it?
Alexis: It's in New York City.
Candice: Why do people go there?
Alexis: It's a good place to relax.

Conversation 2:
Sam: What do you do in your free time?
Devon: I like to jog in the park.
Sam: Why do you do that?
Devon: It's good exercise, and I enjoy being outdoors.
Sam: When are you going next?
Devon: Tomorrow morning. Do you want to come?

Exploring Spoken English

Language Function: Making Small Talk

Track 25   A.   Page 38

Shelli: There are a lot of people here today.
Omar: I'm sorry?
Shelli: I said there are a lot of people at the park today.
Omar: There sure are. It's a beautiful day to be outdoors.
Shelli: It really is. What's the temperature today?
Omar: I don't know, but it feels perfect. I'm here with my son.
Shelli: Oh, which one is your son?
Omar: That's him over there.
Shelli: Really? He's playing with my son!
Omar: That's your son? What's his name?
Shelli: Robert. And my name is Shelli.
Omar: Nice to meet you, Shelli. I'm Omar, and my son is Andy.
Shelli: It's great that the kids can play here.
Omar: It really is.

Track 26   D.   Page 39

A: Everyone's having a good time!
B: What did you say?
A: I said everyone's having a good time.
B: They sure are—it's a fun party!

Unit 3: Treasures from the Past
Lesson A

Building Vocabulary

Track 27   A. Using a Dictionary   Page 44

dishes
exhibit
find

image
looked like
nearby
objects
recently
ruled
tools

Track 28   C. Meaning from Context   Page 44

New Exhibit Opens Today

Queen Cleopatra VII ruled Egypt for fewer than 20 years. People are still very interested in her more than 2000 years later. But until recently, no one knew much about Cleopatra at all. We didn't even know what she looked like because there were no pictures of her.

Now, a new exhibit tells us more about Cleopatra's life. The exhibit has hundreds of objects such as jewelry, tools, and dishes. For the first time we can see Cleopatra's face! There are coins with Cleopatra's image on them.

Developing Listening Skills

Track 29   Pronunciation: The Simple Past Tense *-ed* Word Endings   Page 46

Examples:
look → looked
live → lived
play → played
My grandfather looked like his father.

Examples:
want → wanted
need → needed
start → started
They decided to make a map.

Track 30   Page 46

1. painted
2. explored
3. talked
4. divided
5. closed
6. rested
7. shouted
8. watched

Listening: A Talk about an Ancient City

Track 31   A. Listening for Main Ideas   Page 47

Welcome to the museum and our new exhibit, "Cleopatra: The Search for the Last Queen of Egypt." The objects in this collection come from the ancient city of Alexandria and other nearby cities. Alexandria was one of the richest and greatest cities of the ancient world. Cleopatra lived and ruled there. But the city disappeared nearly 2000 years ago.

Now, archaeologist Franck Goddio has found the lost city of Alexandria. Goddio's new discoveries tell us a lot about Cleopatra's world. Up until a few years ago, we didn't know much about Cleopatra. We knew who her parents were and when she became queen. We knew she was one of the most powerful rulers in Egypt, and that she killed herself.

But there were many things we did not know. Our knowledge of Cleopatra came mostly from legends—old stories that may or may not be true. No one even knew what she looked like. But today, thanks to Goddio and his team, we know much more about her life.

In 1984, Goddio went to Egypt to look for a sunken ship. But he found much more. There in the sand, deep underwater, were the ruins of whole cities. These cities were lost to history. He knew immediately that here were the answers to some of the greatest questions about ancient Egypt. Goddio looked and looked. But these ruins covered a huge area. Goddio couldn't explore them all by himself. He needed a lot of help.

Track 32   B. Note-Taking   Page 47

Welcome to the museum and our new exhibit, "Cleopatra: The Search for the Last Queen of Egypt." The objects in this collection come from the ancient city of Alexandria and other nearby cities. Alexandria was one of the richest and greatest cities of the ancient world. Cleopatra lived and ruled there. But the city disappeared nearly 2000 years ago.

Now, archaeologist Frank Goddio has found the lost city of Alexandria. Goddio's new discoveries tell us a lot about Cleopatra's world. Up until a few years ago, we didn't know much about Cleopatra. We knew who her parents were and when she became queen. We knew she was one of the most powerful rulers in Egypt, and that she killed herself. But there were many things we did not know. Our knowledge of Cleopatra came mostly from legends—old stories that may or may not be true. No one even knew what she looked like. But today, thanks to Goddio and his team, we know much more about her life.

In 1984, Goddio went to Egypt to look for a sunken ship. But he found much more. There in the sand, deep underwater, were the ruins of whole cities. These cities were lost to history. He knew immediately that here were the answers to some of the greatest questions about ancient Egypt. Goddio looked and looked. But these ruins covered a huge area. Goddio couldn't explore them all by himself. He needed a lot of help.

In 1987, Goddio started an organization called the European Institute of Underwater Archaeology. The organization brought together researchers and experts from around the world. Finally, in 1992, Goddio and his team were ready to begin their work. They uncovered statues, containers, musical instruments, tools, and many other objects. They made maps of ancient Alexandria and the two other sunken cities. They explored Cleopatra's palace and the temples where her people prayed to their gods.

Little by little, they brought objects out of the water. Slowly her palace and everything around her came to life before their eyes. For the first time, we can see where Cleopatra lived, where she walked, what she touched. Goddio's team found coins with Cleopatra's image on them. They found statues of gods and goddesses that were in the temples where she walked. They found gold jewelry from her palace. They even found a calendar that people used in her time. Because of Goddio and his team, we are learning more about Cleopatra every day. She is no longer only a legend.

We hope you enjoy your visit to "Cleopatra: The Search for the Last Queen of Egypt."

Lesson B
Building Vocabulary
Track 33   A. Using a Dictionary   Page 54

were made of
carry
everyday
goods
route
sailed
ship
silk
traded
valuable

Track 34   C. Meaning from Context   Page 54
The Shipwreck of an Arab *Dhow*

This is the story of an Arab ship called a *dhow*. The *dhow* left the Middle East, and it sailed east to China. There, the sailors bought everyday objects such as simple dishes, but also valuable goods such as gold and silk. Sadly, the ship sank near Belitung Island in Indonesia, and the sailors never returned home.

Travel was difficult in the ninth century, but not impossible. By land, there was the Silk Road. It was a way for people in one part of the world to trade with people in other parts of the world. By sea, there was the Maritime Silk Route.

Using Vocabulary
Track 35   A.   Page 55
More about the Belitung Dhow

A dhow was a type of ship that was common in the Indian Ocean and the Arabian Sea. *Dhows* were not very large, but they could carry a lot. Around the year 826, one *dhow* sailed from the city of Al Basrah (now Basra, Iraq) to Guangzhou, China. There, the sailors traded with the local people, and they loaded the ship with the new goods they bought.

When the ship left China, it carried thousands of simple dishes and other everyday objects. It also carried silk for making fine clothes, and a few very beautiful and valuable objects. Some of these objects were made of gold. Recently, archaeologists studied the objects, and they think the gold objects were probably gifts for a royal wedding.

The *dhow* chose an unusual route home. Nobody is sure why the sailors took their ship so far south. Because of a storm, or perhaps an accident, the *dhow* sank between two Indonesian islands. Centuries later, in 1999, divers found the dishes and other objects as well as small pieces of the *dhow* itself.

Developing Listening Skills
Listening: A Conversation
Track 36   A. Listening for Main Ideas   Page 56

Patricia: Hey, Chris, what do you think about the homework assignment?

Chris: It sounds pretty easy to me. "Find out more about the Arab *dhow* shipwreck in Indonesia. You can find information on the Internet or at the library. Write a paragraph and bring it to class on Monday."

Patricia: OK . . . I can write a paragraph, but what kind of information can we find?

Chris: Well, you have to think of something.

Patricia: How am I supposed to think of something? I don't really care about the shipwreck, to tell you the truth.

Chris: Hmm . . . maybe you could ask yourself some questions. For example, what did the *dhow* carry from the Middle East to China? They sailed a long way, and they probably had something to trade.

Patricia: Yeah, that's a pretty interesting question. Do you know anything about the goods the ship carried to China?

Chris: No, I have no idea. Another question you could ask is this: Did most ships at that time carry valuable goods such as silk and everyday things such as dishes? Or was this ship special?

Patricia: Special, huh? All right.

Chris: Go ahead, Patricia. Now, you ask some questions.

Patricia: OK, so how did the divers find the shipwreck? Did they just look down one day and there it was?

Chris: Good! See? It's not that hard.

Patricia: And where did the archaeologists come from?

Chris: The archaeologists?

Patricia: Yes, we heard about some archaeologists. They studied the objects from the shipwreck. Were they from Indonesia or some other country?

Chris: That's another interesting question!

Patricia: Oh! I thought of something else. What were the dishes made of?

Chris: Right! Why don't you find some information about that?

Patricia: Yes. And here's another question: How did the Chinese make those beautiful dishes so long ago?

Chris: I see you have a lot of questions!

Patricia: You're right—I do.

Chris: So it'll be no problem to find some information.

Patricia: You're right. Thanks, Chris. I'll see you on Monday!

Chris: See you then. Have a good weekend!

Exploring Spoken English

Track 37   B.   Page 59

Improve Your Memory: Four Easy Steps

Do you remember names, phone numbers, and other information easily? If not, here are some things you can do to improve your memory.

- **Get a good night's sleep.** Getting eight or more hours of sleep can improve your memory and your ability to learn new information by as much as 30 percent.
- **Eat a healthy diet.** Good foods such as fish, olive oil, fruits, and vegetables help your brain stay healthy. A healthy brain means a better memory.
- **Exercise your body.** Any kind of exercise—walking, swimming, playing sports—keeps the blood moving around your body and helps your brain work better.
- **Exercise your mind.** Exercising your brain is helpful. One of the best exercises for your brain is learning a new language.

Unit 4: Weather and Climate
Lesson A
Building Vocabulary

Track 38   A. Using a Dictionary   Page 64

amount
destroy
drought
flooding
forecast
measure
predict
rainfall
storm
temperature

Track 39   C.   Page 64

Water from the Sky: Too Much, or Not Enough?

"How much rain did we get?" It's a question we often hear, and it's important because all life on Earth depends on rainfall. As long as our part of the world gets the usual amount of rain, we're happy.

The problem comes when we get too much rainfall or not enough. In Queensland, Australia, for example, March of 2011 was a month of storms that brought far too much rain. The rain caused flooding in much of the state. Roads were closed, and thousands of people didn't have electricity.

That same spring, very little rain fell in eastern Africa. That caused drought in Somalia, Kenya, and Ethiopia. The terrible conditions destroyed food crops, which couldn't grow without water. There was little grass for animals as well.

The problems are different when the temperature is cold. Then, it's the amount of snowfall that matters. In February of 2011, a huge snowstorm hit the eastern coast of South Korea. It was the biggest snowfall in South Korea since they began to keep records in 1911!

Because rainfall is so important to us, scientists called meteorologists try to predict the amount of rainfall different parts of the world will receive. To do this, they measure air and ocean temperatures. They also watch weather conditions around the world to see how the air is moving. Meteorologists then make weather forecasts to let us know how much rain to expect. They're not always exactly right, but they do know when we'll probably have large amounts of rain or not enough.

Developing Listening Skills

Listening: A Radio Show

Track 40   A. Listening for Main Ideas   Page 66

Nancy: And welcome back. Now we have Brad Jameson with us in the studio. Brad is a meteorologist and the author of a new book. Tell us what it's called, Brad.

Brad: Thanks, Nancy. It's called *Weather in Your Backyard: The Limits of Forecasting*.

Nancy: Now, Brad, some of us get a little angry when the weather forecast is wrong.

Brad: Well, yes, you're right, Nancy. And, and *unfortunately*, the forecast today was for clouds and cool temperatures, but looking out the studio window, I can see that it is actually raining out there! However, I, I can tell you that we're getting it right more often these days. You have to remember, it's not easy to predict the weather.

Nancy: Uh-huh. In your book, you talk about weather in very specific, small areas—in other words, the weather in our backyard, not the weather in the whole country. Could you, can you give us some examples?

Brad: Sure . . . I have two great examples. The first one was in Vermont in the northeastern United States. A couple planned their wedding for a certain day. And the weather forecast called for good weather during the day, with storms possible late in the evening. Well, the weather was great that day—a little windy, but not bad. And they had a huge tent so that the wedding party, the guests, the tables and chairs—everything was under this big tent. Suddenly, a strong gust of wind hit them—wham! It picked up the whole tent and destroyed it.

Nancy: Oh, my goodness!

Brad: Most of the storms were still far away, but right there in their own backyard, there was a tiny, but terrible little storm.

Nancy: Amazing. You mentioned two examples?

Brad: Right. My favorite story is about how planes can change the weather. A few years ago, a scientist saw a plane fly through a cloud. It made a hole in the cloud, and suddenly, it started snowing! Scientists think that planes lower the temperature of some clouds. This makes it snow for a short time.

Nancy: So, meteorologists can make forecasts about the big picture, that's to say they can give us a general idea of what is going to happen, but they can't predict the exact weather in your location.

Brad: That's right, Nancy. But we know that weather forecasts are very important to a lot of people—farmers, for example. The amount of rainfall is something they need to know. Drought and flooding can destroy their crops, so we measure the temperature and the amount of water in the air. We do our best to give farmers and everyone else a correct weather forecast.

Nancy: Thank you, Brad. Well, that's all the time we have.

Track 41   Pronunciation: Reduced *of*   Page 67

Careful Speech	Fast Speech
a lot of snow	a lot-ə snow
most of my friends	most-ə my friends
a glass of water	a glass-ə water
the rest of the lecture	the rest-ə the lecture

Exploring Spoken English

Language Function: Expressing Likes and Dislikes

Track 42   A.   Page 68

Student: Do you like being a meteorologist?
Meteorologist: Oh, yes. I really like it.
Student: Do people get angry with you when your forecast is wrong?
Meteorologist: Yes, sometimes they do, but that's understandable. Even I hate it when I want to do something outdoors and it rains!
Student: Did you ever work in a weather station?
Meteorologist: Yes. I worked at a station in Antarctica. I loved it!
Student: So you like cold weather then?

Meteorologist: Oh, no. I can't stand it! But Antarctica is very interesting.
Student: I'm actually studying to be a meteorologist.
Meteorologist: Really? That's great!

Lesson B
Building Vocabulary

Track 43   A. Meaning from Context   Page 74

Climate Change

While the weather changes from day to day, the word *climate* refers to common weather patterns over a long time. Let's look at how the earth's climate is changing.

Higher Average Temperatures

Although some days are warm and some are cool, the earth's average temperature is higher now than in the past. With more heat, some plants can now grow in places that used to be too cold.

Melting Ice

Much of the world's water is in the form of ice—polar ice at the north and south poles and glaciers in high mountain areas. With higher average temperatures, much of that ice is melting. We now see bare ground high in the mountains instead of glaciers.

Stronger Storms

The world's oceans are also somewhat warmer than in the past. This means that the right conditions exist for stronger storms, especially hurricanes and typhoons.

Rising Sea Levels

When polar ice and glaciers melt, more water enters the world's oceans and sea levels rise. This means that islands and areas of low land along a country's coast may soon be under water.

Developing Listening Skills

Listening: A Conversation among Friends

Track 44   A. Listening for Main Ideas   Page 76

Douglas: We're so glad you could come for dinner, Eric.
Eric: Thanks for inviting me. I'm always happy to eat dinner with friends.
Lenora: Douglas is right, Eric. We know you're busy when you come to Canada. We're really happy to see you!
Eric: Thank you, Lenora. I smell something good. What are you cooking?
Douglas: It's my specialty—chicken with rice.
Lenora: And I made a salad to go with it. So, Eric, how is life in Greenland these days?
Eric: Oh, you know. Winters are long. I live on the coast, though, so I get to see the ocean every day. That's always nice.
Douglas: I heard that winters in Greenland are somewhat shorter than they used to be—global warming, I guess?
Eric: Yes, that's true. They're calling it "the greening of Greenland."
Lenora: The "greening"? What does that mean?
Eric: Well, the average temperature in Greenland is rising twice as fast as in other places. So, I, now I have a few trees near my house. Trees didn't use to exist in Greenland, you know!

Douglas: So that's good, right?

Eric: Yes, in some ways. We, um, people are growing some vegetables now—cabbage, potatoes, and things like that. And farmers can grow more grass for their animals.

Lenora: Well, Greenland usually has to buy food from other countries, right? Now you can grow your own food instead.

Eric: Yeah, that's true, and more land is opening up every day. The ice is melting, and the land holds the heat from the sun, so more ice melts.

Douglas: And is the pattern the same in the ocean?

Eric: Actually, it is. The ocean holds heat, too—just like the land. But here's the problem: If all of Greenland's ice melts, sea levels will rise 24 feet!

Douglas: Twenty-four feet? We'll all be underwater!

Eric: A lot of us, anyway. But, well . . . the other thing is, under the sea ice we have oil. So people in Greenland think they're going to make a lot of money from this oil.

Lenora: Wow . . . then global warming might be good for Greenland.

Douglas: I'm not sure I agree. When companies get oil from under the ocean, there can be big problems—like oil spills. If oil gets into the ocean, it's bad for plants, animals, and people. And Greenland's cities are all near the coast. People in those cities don't want sea levels to rise.

Eric: Douglas is right, Lenora. There are some things to worry about.

Lenora: Well, let's not worry about them tonight, OK? Who's ready for dinner?

Eric: Dinner sounds great. I'm getting hungry.

Engage: Discussing Ways to Reduce Greenhouse Gases

Track 45 A. Note-Taking Page 80

Boy: Mom, are you worried about global warming?

Woman: I wasn't, until I saw a TV show about it last year. Now I take it very seriously.

Boy: We talked about it in school, but I don't really get it. What exactly is happening?

Woman: Well, it's all about greenhouse gases and the temperature of the earth. We produce carbon dioxide when we burn oil, coal, and gas . . . and when we breathe, of course. We produce methane, another gas, when we mine coal, raise cattle, or grow rice. And there are other gases called CFCs, used in fridges and spray cans, and so on.

Boy: But those things aren't new . . .

Woman: No, they're not. The thing is the population is growing rapidly and we're becoming more and more industrialized. That means more factories producing more greenhouse gases, more cars on the roads, more cattle and rice to feed the people . . . and more greenhouse gases.

Boy: OK, but what does that have to do with the temperature?

Woman: The gases collect in the earth's atmosphere. They let the light from the sun through, but they don't let the heat it produces back out. Just like the glass in a greenhouse for growing plants. That's how they got their name. And they're important to us—without greenhouse gases, the earth would be a very cold place.

Boy: Oh, but now things have gone too far. Is that it?

Woman: Exactly. The amount of carbon dioxide has increased by 25 percent since records began in the 19th century, and the average temperature of the earth has gone up by one degree.

Boy: One degree? That doesn't sound so bad.

Woman: No, it doesn't, but they say the temperature will keep rising if we do nothing to control the amount of greenhouse gases we produce. That would have a big effect on our weather and living conditions.

Boy: Wow, that's terrible! So what can we do about it?

 CD 2

Unit 5: Focus on Food
Lesson A
Building Vocabulary

Track 2 A. Meaning from Context Page 84

1. The puffer fish is a poisonous fish, but the Japanese government will allow certain chefs to prepare it. They know how to make the fish safe to eat.
2. India is not the only country where people like hot foods. There are many other countries, too.
3. Insects are small but very nutritious. They are full of things that your body needs.
4. Many people can't imagine eating insects for dinner. It is a strange thing to think about.
5. I visited a rainforest in Colombia where the local people eat insects called termites.
6. Some people eat only raw foods. They think cooking food makes it less nutritious.
7. Many people eat honey. They like the sweet taste in their mouths.
8. Lingonberries are an unusual fruit. You find them in Sweden and just a few other places.
9. You can hurt yourself if you touch a durian fruit. You need to wear gloves to open it.
10. People in some parts of Asia think large water insects are delicious, so they eat a lot of them.

Developing Listening Skills

Listening: A Talk by an Anthropology Professor

Track 3 A. Listening for Main Ideas Page 86

Professor: So, there we are. I hope you liked the photos. As you can see, my job is quite interesting. I enjoy teaching here at the university, but it's nice to travel, too. As an anthropologist, I travel a lot.

Student 1: Could I ask a question?

Professor: Of course, Jeremy. Go right ahead.

Student 1: OK. In one of your photos, you're eating something with a lot of people in a village. And you're the only outsider there, I mean, you're not from the village yourself. How do you get people to allow you into their lives like that?

Professor: That's a great question. The most important thing, really, is to make friends—to become part of the community. To do that, I eat the same foods as the local people eat. I stay in the same kind of house as the local people. Basically, if the local people do it, I do it, too.

Student 2: Professor Jones?

Professor: Yes . . . another question?

Student 2: Yes, you talked about eating the same foods as the local people. But what if the food is really weird? I mean, if the food is something very strange to you.

Professor: Well, sometimes it is something new to me, but other people eat it, so I can eat it, too!

Student 3: What kinds of unusual foods have you eaten?

Professor: Oh, a lot of things! Honey ants, for example. They have a sweet taste.

Student 3: Ants? You mean you eat insects?

Professor: Yes, they're delicious! People have been eating insects for a long time. They're quite nutritious—they have a lot of protein in them. And people prepare them in a lot of different ways. Really, that's why, that's one reason I love to learn about people and cultures. People everywhere are very smart. Just look at all the things they know about eating. For example, do you know about cassava? Laura, have you heard of cassava?

Student 2: I think it's some kind of starchy vegetable, right?

Professor: That's right, and it's also called yucca or manioc. Anyway, raw cassava can make people sick. But if you cook it, you can eat it like you eat potatoes, or you can even use it to make bread. It's pretty good!

Student 1: Could I ask another question?

Professor: Sure.

Student 1: Do you ever get sick when you eat these new foods?

Professor: Actually, I never get sick when I travel. Maybe I have a very strong stomach. For me, it's something I enjoy. I enjoy talking, laughing, sharing food with people . . . and people surprise me sometimes. Did you know that people in Mexico eat cactus? Try to imagine it: A long, long time ago, there were these people living in the mountains and deserts of Mexico. They probably killed a few animals for food, and ate plants and insects and other things they could find. And there was this plant growing everywhere—it's a kind of cactus called nopal—and one day somebody thought of a way to eat it. Now, most people don't even want to touch a cactus because it has sharp spines that can hurt your fingers. But somebody found a way to cut the spines off the cactus, and there it was! A nutritious food you can could eat raw or cooked!

Student 3: Have you tried eating cactus?

Professor: Many times. It has a very mild flavor. I like it cooked with some cheese. All right, let's talk about the chapter you read for today . . .

Track 4   Pronunciation: *Can* and *Can't*   Page 87

Examples:
I **can** eat it, too.
I **can't** eat any kind of cheese.
You **can** use it to make bread.
You **can't** eat it raw.

Exploring Spoken English

Track 5   Language Function: Expressing Opinions   Page 88

Examples:
In my opinion, trying new foods is a lot of fun.
I think the food in India is very good.
I don't think durian fruit tastes very good.
For me, this dish is too salty.
To me, this dish is too salty.
Personally, I don't like the food at that restaurant.

Track 6   A.   Page 88

1. **Lydia:** I think these fried potatoes are delicious.
   Henri: I don't think they're good for you, though.
   Lydia: You're probably right.
   Henri: Personally, I don't like to eat any fried foods.
2. **Lee:** Do you like the chicken curry?
   Zachary: In my opinion, it's a little too hot.
   Lee: Really? For me, it's perfect.
3. **Natalia:** What are you cooking? It smells great!
   Jenny: It's falafel. It's a vegetarian dish.
   Natalia: Are you making any meat dishes to go with it?
   Jenny: Not tonight. Personally, I think we eat too much meat.

Grammar: *Can* and *Can't*

Track 7   C.   Page 90

Eating Insects: More Common Than You Might Think

Do you like to eat bugs? Some people do, and some people don't. But here's the surprise—even if you don't like eating insects, you are probably eating them anyway.

"It's estimated that the average human eats one pound (around half a kilogram) of insects each year unintentionally," says Lisa Monachelli, director of youth and family programs at New Canaan Nature Center in Connecticut. In the United States, the U.S. Food and Drug Administration (FDA) allows some insects and insect parts in food, as long as they don't make people sick.

For example, for every 3.5 ounces (100 grams), chocolate can have up to 60 insect parts and peanut butter can have 30 insect fragments, according to the FDA. Tomato sauce can't contain more than 30 fly eggs per 3.5 ounces (100 grams).

And food is not the only place you can find insects and insect parts. Cochineal insects give a red or pink coloring to foods, lipsticks, and beverages. The small bugs are listed as "cochineal extract" on the ingredient list. The fact is—you can't always avoid eating insects.

Lesson A and B Viewing: Forbidden Fruit

After Viewing

Track 8   A. Meaning from Context   Page 93

Forbidden Fruit

In this video, hotels in Malaysian Borneo have a problem: Guests like to bring smelly durian fruit into their rooms. Then the hotel staff has to work hard to get rid of the smell. The video uses interesting words to talk about the problem. For example, it says that "hotels are on the front lines of the durian war." Of course, it's not really a war, but there are two sides: the hotels and the guests who bring durian fruit into the rooms. The video also says, "Hotel managers maintain a constant vigil to keep it out." But the managers can't see everything, so when a guest does bring in a durian fruit, there is "a durian alert," and the hotel staff must work quickly to make the room smell good again.

Lesson B

Building Vocabulary

Track 9   Meaning from Context   Page 94

Three Kinds of Restaurants

Sugar Shacks

You can find *sugar shacks* in the Canadian province of Quebec. They're family restaurants, and you can go there in the early spring for good food and maple syrup—a sweet liquid from maple trees. After you finish your pancakes and hot coffee, order some maple taffy—a kind of candy. To make the taffy, a restaurant worker pours warm maple syrup onto cold snow. Then the worker quickly turns the maple syrup with a wooden stick, and the maple taffy is ready to eat!

Dim Sum Restaurants

In English, *dim sum* means, "a little bit of heart." In the United States, San Francisco is a great place to enjoy these small plates of delicious treats—all made with love. Why San Francisco? In the 1800s, many Chinese people moved to California to work. Their neighborhood in San Francisco was the first Chinatown in the United States. Today, there are numerous *dim sum* restaurants in San Francisco. They all serve this traditional Chinese food with a traditional Chinese beverage—hot tea.

Chocolaterías

Which European country makes the best chocolate? People disagree on that, but we do know that Spain was the first European country to buy cacao beans for making chocolate. Cacao arrived in Seville in 1585! Soon after that, Spanish people fell in love with a drink called hot chocolate. Today, you can find cafés called *chocolaterías* all over Spain. They're popular places for friends and families to meet, and some of them are open all night.

Developing Listening Skills

Before Listening

Track 10   Listening for Specific Information   Page 96

Lucky Noodle is a new restaurant on the north side of the city. It's located at 314 Webster Street near the university campus. Students and other busy people will love the quick service at Lucky Noodle, and everyone will love the food. The prices are not bad either. A large bowl of noodle soup is $6.95, and the pan-fried noodles with chicken costs $8.95.

Track 11   Note-Taking   Page 96

OK, now I want to tell you about the cafeteria. It's on the first floor of South Hall. The cafeteria is open to the public, so anyone can go there to eat. However, most of the time you'll find students and university staff in the cafeteria. All right, the cafeteria is open every day from 6:30 A.M. until 7:00 P.M. That means you can eat most of your meals there. And you really should eat in the cafeteria often because students pay a reduced price for food. It only costs $3.50 for breakfast or lunch, or $5.00 for dinner. Of course, if you're not a student, prices are higher.

Listening: A Conversation between Students

Track 12   A. Listening for Main Ideas   Page 96

Roger: So, what do you think of the cafeteria food?
Aaron: It's OK, I guess. It's not like they serve, you know, homemade food.
Roger: That's true.
Aaron: Why do you ask? Don't you like the food?
Roger: Well, to tell you the truth, I think it's *awful*. Even the beverages are bad . . . like that disgusting coffee? Sometimes it's not even a liquid! Yuck!
Aaron: But it is cheap—only five dollars for dinner!
Roger: I know. I guess that's why it's popular. But I really can't eat the food. And they close before I get hungry in the evening.
Aaron: You're not hungry by seven o'clock?
Roger: No. I usually eat dinner around eight or nine o'clock.
Aaron: Hmmm. So what are you going to do? You have to eat!
Roger: Well, there are numerous . . . really, a lot of good restaurants in our neighborhood. And most of them are open pretty late. I mean, you can order dinner at midnight at the Pink Rose Café.
Aaron: Oh, right! The Pink Rose Café has delicious stuff to eat!
Roger: Exactly! I mean, their pasta dishes are great. Even their vegetable soup is a treat.
Aaron: OK, sure. But what about the prices?
Roger: Yeah. Eating at restaurants is more expensive . . .
Aaron: Hey, I have an idea. Let's meet at the cafeteria for lunch tomorrow.
Roger: All right. I can meet you for lunch, but why the cafeteria?
Aaron: Well, I can show you my favorite cafeteria foods, so like, I know what's OK to eat and what not to eat.
Roger: Sure. That would be great.
Aaron: I mean, it is cheap. And you can eat there pretty quickly, so you won't be late for class.
Roger: That's true. So, see you tomorrow for lunch. Around noon?
Aaron: How about 12:15?
Roger: Sounds good. See you tomorrow.
Aaron: See you then. Bye.

Exploring Spoken English

Track 13   A.   Page 98

Mariana: You should really try tacos. They're delicious!
Jen: What are they like?
Mariana: Well, they're made from fresh, warm tortillas—those are like little corn pancakes, but they're not sweet.
Jen: OK. Fresh tortillas sound good.
Mariana: They are! Then we put a little meat and raw onions and other vegetables on top.
Jen: Well, I'll try tacos if you'll try *kim chee*.
Mariana: Hmmm. What's *kim chee*?
Jen: It's made from raw vegetables with salt, red chili, and fish sauce. Then, we wait several days before we eat it.
Mariana: Really? It doesn't sound very good to me.
Jen: Oh, it's great! You only eat a little, and you have it with other food such as rice or soup.
Mariana: I could try it, I guess.
Jen: Yes, try it! And I'll try tacos.

Unit 6: Housing
Lesson A
Building Vocabulary

Track 14   A. Using a Dictionary   Page 104

apartments
balcony
building
comfortable
residents
roof
spacious
stairs
style
walls

Track 15   C.   Page 104

Casa Milà

In Barcelona, Spain, both visitors and residents of the city know about the architect Antoni Gaudí. The Casa Milà is perhaps his best-known building. From the outside, the walls look like natural stone. On the roof, several large, unusual works of art are actually chimneys—they carry away gases from cooking and heating from inside the apartments.

Casa Batlló

The Casa Batlló is another of Gaudí's apartment buildings. The outside of the building is very colorful, and it's easy to see that Gaudi was an artist as well as an architect. Not every apartment is spacious, but each apartment has a balcony, so residents can stand outside their bedrooms or living rooms and see the street below.

Park Güell

One of the most popular Gaudí sites isn't a building at all. The Park Güell is a large outdoor park, but Gaudí's architectural style is everywhere—from the stairs and stone columns to the beautiful artwork. There are comfortable places to sit, and the trees and gardens invite city residents to relax and enjoy nature.

Developing Listening Skills
Before Listening

Track 16   A.   Page 106

Mrs. Ferrer: I don't want to live in that neighborhood.
Mr. Ferrer: Why not? It's close to your office.
Mrs. Ferrer: Yes, but there's a lot of congestion. Everyone is looking for a place to park their cars, and it's hard just to cross the street sometimes.
Mr. Ferrer: So where do you want to live?
Mrs. Ferrer: I like the demographics in Riverdale. There are a lot of young families with good jobs there.
Mr. Ferrer: OK, but we're getting older, and our children live on their own now.
Mrs. Ferrer: True, but we're not geriatric yet. We're still young enough to enjoy a nice neighborhood.
Mr. Ferrer: Then we'll ask the real estate agent to show us apartments in Riverdale.
Mrs. Ferrer: Good. I think we'll like it there.

Listening: A PowerPoint Presentation

Track 17   A. Listening for Main Ideas   Page 107

Marco Nadal: OK, I think we can begin. Good morning, everyone. My name is Marco Nadal, and I'm a real estate developer. First, thank you for coming. Since all of you are real estate agents, I want to give you some information about a completely new apartment complex. It's called La Costa—The Coast, in English. And it *is* on the coast. It's in the popular Barceloneta neighborhood, so it's close to downtown, and even better—it's right on the beach!

I have some slides to show you. OK. In this first slide, you see the three buildings in the complex. They're high-rise buildings, and each building has 22 floors. In all, there are 240 apartments! We have something for all of your clients, and we hope you bring many of them to see La Costa.

The apartments are comfortable and spacious. Most of them have one or two balconies, except for the one-bedroom apartments. But all of the residents can use the swimming pool. It's on the roof of building number two. Let's look at the next slide. There! Who needs a balcony when you can see the ocean from this rooftop swimming pool?

All right. The next slide shows the lobby of building number three. As you can see, the style is modern, and it's very "Barcelona." One wall is covered with art. It's a colorful mosaic made of small pieces of glass—thousands of pieces. And look carefully—it's a scene from Park Güell—beautiful, isn't it? Are there any questions?
Real Estate Agent 1: Yes, I have a question. Many of my clients are families with children. Is the La Costa apartment complex a good place for them?
Marco Nadal: Definitely! The Barceloneta neighborhood is popular with families. There are good schools, and of course we're close to the beach. The La Costa complex welcomes children, so please, do bring families to see these apartments. Any other questions?
Real Estate Agent 2: Yes, in the last slide, I see some stairs. Of course, there must be elevators in high-rise apartment buildings. Could you tell me how many elevators there are in each building?
Marco Nadal: Certainly. The stairs go up to the restaurant and some small shops. But we have four elevators in each building for the residents to use. In addition, there is one large service elevator in each building. That's helpful for moving furniture and things like that. If there are no more questions, I'll give you some information about prices. The cost of the apartments is really very low.

Exploring Spoken English
Language Function: Agreeing and Disagreeing

Track 18   B.   Page 109

Sasha: I'm so happy! I finally found a new place.
Janet: That's great! Where are you living?
Sasha: I'm living on the east side, and it's close to a bus line.
Janet: Being close to the bus line is good, but the east side is dangerous.
Sasha: That's a good point, but I think the neighborhood is improving.
Janet: Really? What's happening there?

Sasha: They're putting in better lighting, so the streets aren't so dark at night.
Janet: That's good.
Sasha: My new apartment is also in a safe building, and that's important.
Janet: I agree.

Lesson A and B Viewing: Don't Believe Your Eyes!

Before Viewing

Track 19   B. Using a Dictionary   Page 112

This video is about a kind of art called *trompe l'oeil*. It's a painting technique that is popular in an Italian village called Camogli. There, many people have *trompe l'oeil* paintings of windows, balconies, flowers, and even animals on the outside walls of their houses.

Houses in Camogli have always been colorful. In the past, fishermen wanted to see their houses from the sea, so they painted the houses in bright colors. Nowadays, people think the *trompe l'oeil* paintings make the houses look beautiful and grand.

These days, only a few artists know how to do *trompe l'oeil*, so some people worry about Camogli losing this tradition. Artists Raffaella Stracca and Carlo Pere are keeping the *trompe l'oeil* tradition alive, however. If you ever go to Camogli, take a careful look around. Things are not always what they seem to be.

Lesson B

Building Vocabulary

Track 20   A. Using a Dictionary   Page 114

belong
build
damage
deserts
especially
locations
population
property
rapid
tourists

Using Vocabulary

Track 21   A.   Page 115

Vacation Homes: Owning a Piece of Paradise

Q: What are vacation homes?
A: They're usually houses or condominiums. Families only use these homes during vacations, so they want them to be in beautiful locations.
Q: Why is Baja California popular for vacations?
A: It has coasts on the Pacific Ocean and the Sea of Cortez, so tourists can enjoy sea life such as dolphins, whales, and unusual fish. Its beautiful mountains and deserts are also excellent for hiking and sightseeing.
Q: Can anyone own a home in Baja California?
A: Yes. You don't have to be a Mexican citizen to own property here. Many vacation homes belong to people from other countries, especially Canada and the United States.

Q: Are there a lot of new vacation homes for sale?
A: Yes. Most of Baja California's population lives in the north, in cities such as Tijuana and Mexicali. Recently, though, there has been rapid growth in the south, especially near Cabo San Lucas and La Paz. They want to build a lot of new houses and hotels quickly in those places.
Q: Is everyone happy about the housing growth?
A: No. Some people worry about damage to the environment as more and more people move in. Baja California is also very dry, so having enough drinking water for everyone is another concern.

Developing Listening Skills

Track 22   Pronunciation: Contractions with *Be*   Page 116

Examples:

I am	I'm
You are	You're
He is	He's
She is	She's
It is	It's
That is	That's
We are	We're
They are	They're
There is	There's

Listening: A Conversation

Track 23   A. Listening for Main Ideas   Page 117

Gretchen: Honey, did you read this article about Egypt?
Michael: No, I didn't. What does it say?
Gretchen: It says that the population of Egypt is growing.
Michael: Uh-huh.
Gretchen: It's a pretty rapid increase—about 1.5 million people every year.
Michael: Wow—that is fast.
Gretchen: And most people in Egypt live near the Nile River.
Michael: Right. I think they always have. That's where the water is, so it's the best location for houses and cities.
Gretchen: And farms, too. The rest of the country is desert, so they grow a lot of food along the Nile.
Michael: Uh-huh.
Gretchen: Now, though, the Egyptian government has a plan to "green" the desert, especially the desert between Cairo and Alexandria.
Michael: How do you "green" the desert?
Gretchen: That's the interesting part. The government is building houses and roads and things. They're also selling property there at a low price.
Michael: That's great, but how does it make the desert green?
Gretchen: It doesn't, but they're moving water from the Nile to the "new land," so farmers can go there and grow food, and other people can build houses there. Anyway, it's a lot greener than it used to be, and people are living there now.
Michael: Living on new land, huh? That *is* pretty interesting.
Gretchen: Yeah, but not everyone is happy about it.
Michael: Hmmm. Let me guess. They're doing some kind of damage to the environment?
Gretchen: Well, it does take a lot of energy to move water, but the real problem is the water itself. Not everyone agrees who it belongs to.

Michael: The water belongs to Egypt, right? That's where the Nile River is.

Gretchen: It's in other countries, too.

Michael: Oh, I see what you mean.

Gretchen: And some people think it's better to leave the desert alone—not do anything. They think tourists could visit Egypt to see the desert—you know—the natural desert.

Michael: Yeah, but tourists already go to Egypt, I think. And the population of Egypt needs places to live.

Gretchen: That's true.

Exploring Spoken English

Track 24   A.   Page 118

Straw Houses: Another Way to "Go Green"

What is your house made of? Building a house from concrete or metal requires large amounts of energy and pollutes the air. Building a house from wood means cutting down trees and damaging the environment.

Builder Michael Furbish has another idea: Use straw to make buildings. "Most other building materials require a lot of energy use in production and manufacturing at a factory," explains Furbish. Straw is a kind of grass, and it takes little energy to grow. It's not very nutritious for animals, however, so farmers normally dry it and use it for animals to sleep on.

After the straw is dry, farmers use a machine to make bales—large rectangular bricks of straw. Then, builders such as Furbish build walls with the bales. When they finish the walls, they cover them with plaster inside and outside. That keeps out water as well as insects and small animals.

Furbish used about 900 straw bales for his family's two-story, three-bedroom house. His company used about 4000 bales to build an elementary school in Maryland, USA.

Do you think a straw-bale house is for you? You won't know until you try living in one, but for Furbish, it's a greener way to build.

Unit 7: Exploring Space
Lesson A
Building Vocabulary

Track 25   A. Using a Dictionary   Page 124

ago
amazing
appears
atmosphere
become
even
gas
gravity
in contrast
lasted

Track 26   B. Meaning from Context   Page 124

A Look at the Stars

Here on Earth, we like to look up at the stars in the night sky. In space, the stars look even more amazing!

Astronaut Don Thomas flew into space on the space shuttle *Columbia*. He said later, "I could see many more stars. I also could see stars of different colors. Some are white. Others are blue, red, or yellow like our sun."

For most of us, stars in the night sky appear to twinkle. That's because light from the stars travels through the earth's atmosphere before we see it. Gases in the atmosphere are always moving, and that makes the light from the stars look unsteady. In contrast, "They don't twinkle in space," says Thomas. "They look like steady points of light." Our own sun is a yellow, average-sized star. It formed around 4.6 billion years ago—probably in a very large cloud of gas and dust called a nebula. Bits of gas and dust came together, and then gravity began to pull the gas and dust into a ball. As the ball grew larger, its gravity grew stronger. Over time, the gravity became so strong that the ball collapsed and the gas heated up. A star was born!

Stars last a very long time—for millions or even billions of years. Our sun will get cooler and die someday, but it won't happen any time soon.

Developing Listening Skills

Track 27   Pronunciation: Contractions with Will   Page 126

Examples:
I'll see you tomorrow.
You'll really like that movie.
She'll tell us about the assignment soon.
Do you know when he'll get here?
Just think, next week we'll be in Hawaii!
After the plane takes off, they'll bring us something to drink.

Track 28   A.   Page 126

1.	I'll	I'll be home by eight thirty.
2.	You'll	I know you'll enjoy this book.
3.	He'll	He'll call you when he gets to Geneva.
4.	She'll	She'll finish the project by the end of the week.
5.	They'll	They'll have to wait in line to buy their tickets.
6.	We'll	We'll come and visit you as soon as we can.

Listening: A Presentation by a Medical Doctor

Track 29   A. Checking Predictions   Page 127

Dr. Carter: Hi, everyone. I'm Dr. Carter. I'm a medical doctor, and I work for the space program. First, thank you for inviting me to your class today. I always enjoy talking to children about space exploration. I also brought a video about life in space, and you'll see that in a few minutes.

First, you probably want to know why a doctor works for the space program. Well, astronauts need to be in good physical health. Seven years ago, I spent a month on the International Space Station. It was an amazing time in my life, and I learned a lot about staying healthy in space.

The most important thing to know is that space is *not* a good place for human beings to live. It's much too cold for us, and there's no atmosphere, so there's no air to breathe. And here on Earth, the atmosphere pushes down on us all the time. That air pressure is very important to us. With no air and no air pressure, a person can't even live for 10 minutes!

Fortunately, astronauts have spacesuits. Spacesuits protect the body, and they also provide air and air pressure. In the video, you'll see an astronaut *outside* the space station. That's called a "space walk," and astronauts can do space walks thanks to their spacesuits. In contrast, they can wear everyday clothes *inside* the space station. There are gases such as nitrogen and oxygen inside, so it's pretty much like the air on Earth.

In the video, we'll see the astronauts doing everyday things such as eating and sleeping. Astronauts on the space station eat five small meals every day. Most of the food is frozen or canned, so it lasts longer than fresh food, but it might not taste quite as good. When it's time to sleep, you'll see that it's light outside the station. In fact, when you're on the space station, the sun rises and sets several times in 24 hours, so many astronauts don't get enough sleep. For some of them, it's helpful to cover the windows. That way, it appears to be nighttime, and it's easier to sleep.

The last thing I'll talk about is "zero gravity." In the video, the astronauts almost appear to be flying inside the space station. That's because the station is moving very fast, so really, the astronauts are always falling. It feels like there's no gravity, and it's kind of fun. Unfortunately, people lose muscle in zero gravity because their bodies don't need to work very hard. Astronauts can become thin and weak, so they need to exercise for two or three hours every day to stay strong and healthy. All right! Your teacher is going to turn off the lights, and we're going to watch the video. I hope you like it.

Exploring Spoken English

Track 30   C.   Page 129

The Future of Space Exploration

Interviewer: Dr. Takei, when do you think humans will live on Mars?
Dr. Takei: That's an interesting question. Mars is a cold planet. If astronauts go to Mars, they'll need spacesuits to stay warm. And even though Mars has some atmosphere, it's not like the air on Earth. Those spacesuits will need to provide oxygen and air pressure, too.
Interviewer: I see, but I've read articles about this. They say we can make Mars more like Earth.
Dr. Takei: Yes, that's probably true. There is ice on Mars, and the atmosphere is mostly carbon dioxide. That's a greenhouse gas, and if you add a few things to it, it's going to begin to warm the planet.
Interviewer: Global warming on Mars?
Dr. Takei: Yes, that's the idea—global warming to melt the ice on Mars. However, oxygen is still going to be a problem. Some scientists think that future astronauts will bring plants to Mars to make oxygen—simple plants at first, but over time, even trees could grow!
Interviewer: That's amazing! But what's your opinion? Will any of this really happen?
Dr. Takei: In my opinion, it won't happen during our lives, or any time soon. Space exploration is expensive, and right now, countries don't have the money. It also takes a lot of time. It could take 1000 years to make Mars more like Earth!

Lesson A and B Viewing: Exploration of the Solar System

Before Viewing

Track 31   B. Using a Dictionary   Page 132

The last people to walk on the moon were the crew of *Apollo 17* in 1972. By that time, however, unmanned space exploration of the planets in our solar system was already taking place.

Sending satellites and probes into space is safer and less expensive than sending people. Probes have been sent to the sun, to other planets, and to their moons. Mars alone has been studied by a dozen space probes. The probes either fly by or orbit a planet, and they send pictures and other valuable information back to Earth.

Lesson B

Building Vocabulary

Track 32   A. Meaning from Context   Page 134

Telescopes of the Past

As far as we know, Galileo was the first astronomer to observe the moon, planets, and stars through a telescope. In the seventeenth century, telescopes were just glass lenses inside tubes made of wood. The lenses were shaped by hand to make things appear larger. Soon, however, people wanted bigger telescopes to be able to see farther into space. Large glass lenses were heavy and didn't work well in a telescope, so in 1668, Isaac Newton invented something new: a telescope that used a mirror to reflect light. Soon, reflecting telescopes became the first choice for astronomers.

Telescopes of the Present

As telescopes became larger, it became necessary to put them inside some kind of building. Observatories, buildings with telescopes inside for doing research, were built as early as in the eighteenth century. With these larger telescopes, astronomers discovered planets that Galileo never knew about—Uranus and Neptune.

Three of today's largest observatories stand on top of Mauna Kea in Hawaii. At nearly 14,000 feet (4300 meters), Mauna Kea is above 40 percent of the earth's atmosphere. The Keck Observatory is among the observatories on Mauna Kea, and the mirrors in its two reflecting telescopes are 33 feet (10 meters) across! Their size allows astronomers to see far into space.

Telescopes of the Future

The Hubble Space Telescope was not the first telescope in space, but it is large, and it is completely outside the earth's atmosphere. Hubble can reach farther into space and view more kinds of objects in space than any telescope before it. Work on newer, larger telescopes is also happening here on Earth. The Large Synoptic Survey Telescope will be able to view a wide area of space instead of the narrow area of older telescopes. And the Giant Magellan Telescope will be able to collect four times as much light as the telescopes on Mauna Kea.

Developing Listening Skills

Before Listening

Track 33   A.   Page 136

Tour Guide: All right. Before we see the telescope, we'll visit our museum exhibit. It's not very big, but it has some interesting old photos inside. First, please look at this group of people. Do you recognize any of them?

Tourist 1: That's Albert Einstein!
Tour Guide: Right. This picture was taken in 1921—several years after Einstein wrote his famous books about relativity. The next photo shows the observatory in 1892.

Listening: A Talk by a Tour Guide

Track 34   A. Listening for Main Ideas   Page 137

Tour Guide: Welcome, everyone, and thank you for coming to the Yerkes Observatory. Our tour will last about 45 minutes. Before we go inside, please take a look at this beautiful building. It's from the 1890s, so it's among the oldest observatories in North America. And what do you think makes the Yerkes telescope special? Anyone?
Tourist 1: Is it the size?
Tour Guide: It *is* the size! The Yerkes telescope is the largest refracting telescope in the world. Of course, there are much larger telescopes nowadays, but they're *reflecting* telescopes. They use mirrors to collect light. Who can tell me what a refracting telescope uses?
Tourist 2: I think I know this. It uses lenses, right?
Tour Guide: Absolutely right! The telescope at Yerkes uses two large, 40-inch glass lenses. With this telescope, scientists can observe the moon, planets, and even other galaxies. OK, let's go inside.
Tour Guide: All right. Before we see the telescope, we'll visit our museum exhibit. It's not very big, but there are some interesting old photos. First, please look at this group of people. Do you recognize anyone?
Tourist 1: That's Albert Einstein!
Tour Guide: Right. This picture was taken in 1921—several years after Einstein wrote his famous books about relativity. The next photo shows the observatory in 1892. As you can see, there was nothing around it. It was out in the country and high on a hill, so astronomers could view the night sky.

OK, I know you want to see the telescope. We'll need to go up some stairs in order to reach it, and the building is old, so there's no elevator. They didn't think an elevator was necessary back then. Please let me know if anyone needs help.

Well, this is it! You'll notice an opening—kind of like a window—up there. That's so the scientists can use the telescope to see outside.
Tourist 2: Excuse me, but that's pretty small. How do the scientists see other parts of the sky? Does the opening move?
Tour Guide: Actually, the whole room turns completely around! After my talk, I'll show you how it works. So, maybe you're asking yourselves, "What can astronomers see through the Yerkes telescope?" In fact, they can see a lot, and they've made some important discoveries here. For example, they discovered the shape of our own galaxy, the Milky Way. Before that, we didn't know that the Milky Way has a spiral shape, with arms . . . sort of like a starfish . . .

Exploring Spoken English

Grammar

Track 35   B. Using a Dictionary   Page 138

The Dark-Sky Movement

Most of the world's people now live in or near cities, where doing most things at night is as easy as doing them during the day.

Seeing the stars at night, however, is not easy to do in a city. Streetlights and lights from businesses and advertisers shine into the night sky, and only the brightest stars can be seen.

The dark-sky movement wants to change this. They argue that seeing the night sky is important for everyone—not only for astronomers. They say that outdoor lighting affects human health and wildlife, and they recommend simple things such as streetlights that only let light shine down at the street, not up at the sky.

Track 36   C.   Page 139

Yoshi: Hi, Tim. What are you reading?
Tim: It's information about a star party.
Yoshi: A star party? Is that a party with a lot of movie stars or something?
Tim: No, Yoshi. At star parties, people get together to look at the night sky.
Yoshi: Do you need to go to a party to do that?
Tim: Well, they're going to a national park. It's far from any cities.
Yoshi: I see . . . so there are no city lights nearby.
Tim: Exactly. People say it's a lot of fun. Do you want to go?
Yoshi: Maybe. When?
Tim: The bus leaves at five o'clock on Friday afternoon, and it gets to the park around seven thirty.
Yoshi: What time does the bus get back here?
Tim: It gets back pretty late—around midnight. What do you think?
Yoshi: It sounds like fun. Let's go!

 CD 3

Unit 8: Art and Music
Lesson A
Building Vocabulary

Track 2   A. Using a Dictionary   Page 144

conscious of
constantly
copies
forever
huge
public
repeat
sculptures
solid
temporary

Using Vocabulary

Track 3   D.   Page 145

Artist Profile: Jason deCaires Taylor
Background: Taylor grew up in Asia and Europe. As a child, he often swam among Malaysia's coral reefs—places where small sea animals and plants grow on rocks or other solid objects on the ocean floor. Reefs are important for many kinds of ocean life, but they're in trouble because of fishing and climate change.
Recent Project: These days, Taylor still likes to swim, and he is conscious of the need to help ocean reefs and ocean life. His recent art project does exactly that.

The Silent Evolution is a group of sculptures. Taylor used real people as models when he was making them. In a way, all the sculptures are copies of people, and they look just like them.

The sculptures are in a public place, but they are not easy to see. They are on the ocean floor near Cancún, Mexico. There are more than 400 of them, and together, they form one huge piece of art. It's especially interesting because the artist did not repeat any of the sculptures—each one is a sculpture of a different person.

The Future: Taylor's artwork is constantly changing. Sea animals and plants make their homes on the sculptures just as they do on natural reefs, and in time, a new reef will form. That means the sculptures are temporary, and if you want to see them, you need to do it soon. Taylor hopes the new reef that forms over the sculptures will last forever, or at least far into the future.

Developing Listening Skills

Listening: A PowerPoint Presentation

Track 4   A. Note-Taking   Page 146

Professor: Welcome back, everyone. As you remember, last week we talked about art in the 20th century. Today we're changing topics. I want to talk about art that you won't find in a museum. That's because it's temporary art—temporary because it's not supposed to last forever, only for a short time. Let's look at my first slide. Can everyone see it? What kind of animal is this?

Student 1: It looks like a dragon.

Professor: That's right. It's a friendly-looking dragon. But this sculpture is not made from something solid like stone. Can you see what it's made from?

Student 2: I think it's snow!

Professor: It is snow, and it looks like a sunny day, so the sculpture is not going to last—it's snow, so it's going to melt. This snow sculpture is part of a winter festival in Montreal, Canada, and sculptures like this—made from snow, or cheese, or even chocolate—are nothing new. They're popular at festivals, and they tell us two important things about temporary art. First, we often see it outdoors. Instead of sitting in an art museum, temporary art is often done in public places. In this case, it's a public street.

And second, look closely at this picture. Do you see the crowd of people around the sculpture? Temporary art brings people together.

In my next slide, you'll see an artist in Madrid, Spain. He's working on a copy of a famous painting—the *Mona Lisa*, right? But he's not working with paint; he's working with chalk. He's working outdoors in a public place, and people are coming to watch him work. What else do you notice?

Student 1: I see some money. There are coins on the street.

Professor: That's right. Artists and other creative people need to make a living. Temporary art, outdoors in public places, brings people together because it's fun. It's interesting to watch the artist work, and people will pay for that. Of course, rain and people's feet will damage this piece because it is outdoors.

Now, not every artist wants to attract a crowd of people. Let's look at my third slide. Here, you see a huge piece of sand art in California in the United States. These circles in the sand repeat, getting larger and larger as the artist moves farther out.

Next slide. And here is the artist, Jim Denevan. He works alone, and it usually takes him about seven hours to finish a piece. While he is working, he is constantly moving and making marks in the sand. And when he is finished, well . . . the ocean tides soon erase Denevan's work. He is conscious of this, of course, but it doesn't seem to bother him. Like any temporary art, Denevan's work doesn't last forever.

Exploring Spoken English

Grammar: Modals of Possibility and Probability

Track 5   A.   Page 148

Conversation 1:

Amy: Hmm. Wanda isn't answering her phone.

Bill: She didn't answer my email yesterday, either.

Amy: She must be out of town. She usually answers her phone.

Bill: Right . . . she could be in Osaka.

Conversation 2:

Reggie: Who is the man over there near the door?

Jenna: He might be Ann's father, but I'm not sure.

Reggie: No, he can't be Ann's father. He's too young.

Jenna: We could go over there and ask him.

Reggie: Yes, but he might not want to talk to us now. It looks like he's leaving.

Language Function: Speculating about a Situation

Track 6   A.   Page 149

Are These Elephants Really Artists?

You might think the paintings are beautiful, or you might not, but you have to admit they're unusual. They're elephant paintings, and some of them cost thousands of dollars.

Elephant art began at zoos in the United States. Zookeepers there saw an elephant named Ruby using a stick to make marks in the dirt. They bought paints and brushes for her, and soon she was painting. In a book about Ruby, author Dick George says she loved to paint, and she even chose the colors.

In Thailand, the Thai Elephant Conservation Center (TECC) now teaches elephants to paint. They think it might be good for them. The animals learn to hold the paintbrush, and trainers help them to move their trunks and paint pictures. Some paintings show real things such as flowers, trees, and even elephants, but according to the TECC, the elephants don't understand the pictures. They just follow the instructions of their trainers.

But some people think there could be more to it than that. Different elephants have their own painting styles, and their paintings become more detailed over time. And to people who buy the paintings, some elephants are better painters than others. For example, an elephant named Ramona may be the most famous elephant in Bali. Many people buy her paintings, and she seems to have an artist's personality. Ramona likes to work with dark colors. She also stops and looks at a painting carefully before choosing the next color, and she only paints when she wants to paint.

Lesson B

Building Vocabulary

Track 7   A. Using a Dictionary   Page 154

afford
album
appeal
award
interpret
lively
lyrics
perform
simple
song

Track 8   C.   Page 154

1. We saved our money for a long time, and now we can afford to buy a piano. We have enough money.
2. The show was fun and the music was lively, so everyone wanted to dance.
3. It's a simple piece of music, so it was easy for my son to learn.
4. It's good music, but I can't understand the lyrics. Can you understand the words?
5. She's going to perform at the Tango Club. You'll need to buy a ticket if you want to hear her.
6. You can download just one song. That costs less than downloading the whole album.
7. The trumpet can be a loud instrument, but its sound appeals to me. I really like it.
8. He interprets popular songs in an interesting way. He plays them in his own way.
9. They're playing at a classical music competition. There are several awards for the best musicians.

Using Vocabulary

Track 9   B.   Page 155

David: Listen. . . . Do you know the name of this song?
Helena: It's called, *What a Wonderful World.*
David: I like it. I think I'll buy it online.
Helena: You should buy the whole album. There are a lot of good songs on it.

Mitch: This music is really lively—it makes me want to get up and dance!
Joaquin: Well, in my opinion, they're playing it too fast.
Mitch: That's the way these musicians interpret the song. It's just their style.
Joaquin: Yes, but it doesn't appeal to me. I prefer calmer music.

Lila: I love this song! Let's sing it together.
Julie: I can't. I don't know the lyrics.
Lila: That's OK. You can read them right here.
Julie: The words are pretty small, but I can see them. OK, let's sing!

Developing Listening Skills

Listening: Radio Program

Track 10   A. Critical Thinking   Page 156

DJ Brian Johnson: This is Radio KBLM, and I'm your host, Brian Johnson. You've just heard a lively piece of music by the great ukulele player Jake Shimabukuro. It's from his new album *Peace, Love, & Ukulele.*

Now, you're probably asking yourself, "Ukulele music? Why are we listening to ukulele music?" Actually, that's a pretty good question. It's not the kind of music we usually play on this radio station. But Shimabukuro is not your usual ukulele player, either.

Let me give you a little background information. Shimabukuro is from Hawaii, and in Hawaii, the ukulele is a big part of the culture. He has performed his music since 1998, and in 1999, he won an award called the Na Hoku Hanohano Award for his work with two other musicians. Soon after that, Shimabukuro left the trio and began his solo career. He has become very popular on the Internet, where you can download his songs, or if you can't afford music downloads, you can watch videos of his performances for free. You'll see him playing the ukulele by himself—he's not a singer, so the songs have no lyrics—and you'll hear some of the best ukulele playing in the world.

OK, as I said, Shimabukuro is not new to the world of music, and *Peace, Love, & Ukulele* is the ninth album he has made since 1999. But this album is different because Shimabukuro doesn't play alone, and here's the reason: The ukulele is a pretty simple instrument. It's small and only has four strings. Most of the time, when Shimabukuro performs, he plays popular songs that the audience already knows—songs by Michael Jackson, or the rock band Queen, or George Harrison from the Beatles. He has to interpret the music in his own way because he can't play every note on the ukulele. He says the audience hears the rest of the song in their heads—the parts that he isn't playing. But this album has some new songs on it that Shimabukuro wrote. The audience hasn't heard the songs before, so he wanted a fuller sound—with drums and bass and other musical instruments.

Trust me—you will want to hear this album. Shimabukuro plays several different styles of music, so whether you like rock music or classical music or traditional Hawaiian songs, something on this album will appeal to you.

OK, let's hear a little more from Jake Shimabukuro . . .

Pronunciation

Track 11   Linking Final Consonants to Vowel Sounds   Page 157

Separate words: *This – is – Rebecca. She – has – eight – ukuleles – at – home.*
Linked words: *This is Rebecca. She has eight ukuleles at home.*

Examples:
afford any
good example
book about
move over

Track 12   A.   Page 157

1. ten artists
2. violin music
3. favorite song
4. beautiful evening
5. they're outdoors
6. Portuguese immigrants
7. good album
8. rolled under
9. interesting lyrics
10. gave it

Track 13   C.   Page 157

He has performed his music since 1998, and in 1999, he won an award called the Na Hoku Hanohano Award for his work with two other musicians. Soon after that, Shimabukuro left the trio and began his solo career. He has become very popular on the Internet, where you can download his songs, or if you can't afford music downloads, you can watch videos of his performances for free.

Exploring Spoken English

Grammar: Modals of Necessity

Track 14   C.   Page 159

My name is Alicia, and I live in the state of Guanajuato in central Mexico. Here in Guanajuato, music and dancing are a big part of life. There are a lot of festivals here, and many kinds of music, but my favorite kind of music is traditional Mexican music—the kind of music my grandparents and great-grandparents listened to.

I'm a folk dancer, and I love to perform at special events. To be a folk dancer, you have to love the culture and the music here. That's the most important thing, but we also need to work hard and practice a lot. We dance in groups, and every person has to know the steps. And you can't buy traditional folk dancing dresses at the store, so we have to make our own. We wear traditional dresses that only come from this part of Mexico.

Unit 9: Our Relationship with Nature
Lesson A

Building Vocabulary

Track 15   A. Using a Dictionary   Page 164

ahead
depend
hunt
raise
relationship
respect
responsibility
share
value
within

Track 16   B. Meaning from Context   Page 164

The Maasai People and Cattle

The Maasai people of East Africa have a special relationship with one kind of animal. They depend on cattle for meat and milk, which make up most of the Maasai diet. In order to raise cattle in a dry climate, the Maasai people share land. Each family has its own animals, but they move the cattle over long distances and onto different families' land in order to find enough grass for the cattle to eat.

The Sami People and Reindeer

Like the Maasai, the Sami people of northern Europe value one animal more than any other. In this difficult climate, reindeer give the Sami people food, clothing, and other useful items. Nowadays, some Sami people raise reindeer on farms, but many Sami people still travel long distances with their animals. This gives them a detailed knowledge of the land and a great respect for nature. No one knows exactly what is ahead for the Sami people because climate change makes the future of the Arctic uncertain.

Using Vocabulary

Track 17   B. Meaning from Context   Page 165

The Australian Aborigines and Australian Animals

The Aborigines of Australia have a different kind of relationship with animals. Australia has many kinds of animals, and all of them are part of the Aborigines' traditional culture. In the past, they hunted some of the animals for food. Other animals appeared in stories or in very old paintings on rocks.

For the Aborigines, everything in nature is connected, and human beings have a special role within the natural world. One group of Aborigines believes it is their responsibility to make sure Australia's kangaroos are doing well.

Developing Listening Skills
Listening: A Lecture

Track 18   A. Listening for Main Ideas   Page 167

Professor: All right, today we're going to continue our discussion on ethics. We'll discuss the question, "Should the Inuit people of North America be allowed to hunt seals?" It's an important question, and in recent years, the European Union made it illegal to trade seal products. So in Europe, you can't buy or sell seal skins, or seal oil, or anything made from seals.

Now, you probably don't wear seal-skin clothing or use a lot of seal oil, right? And the law is popular with most people in Europe. Why? Because they see pictures of cute baby seals, and then they see pictures of the seal hunt. People kill the seals with a gun, or in the more old-fashioned way, by hitting them on the head. The pictures show the red blood on the ice, and for many people, it's disgusting. They think it's their responsibility to stop the seal hunt.

Yes? You have a question?

Student 1: Yes, I have seen those pictures—and videos, too. They're really difficult to watch! I'm not surprised that Europeans want to stop seal hunting! It's awful!

Professor: It does look bad, but the Inuit people have a different opinion. They depend on animals for food. After all, not many plants can grow in such a cold climate, so people there can't raise crops such as rice or wheat. Therefore, the Inuit people have a special relationship with animals. They say they value the animals and have a lot of respect for them, and with seals, they know how to kill the animals quickly. They compare it to Europeans and other people killing animals such as chickens or cattle for food. Of course, a lot of us don't see those animals being killed, so maybe that's why it doesn't upset us.

Anyway, how does the law in the European Union affect hunters in North America? Well, it doesn't affect a lot of the hunters. Many of the people in those pictures and videos are not Inuit people. They hunt seals for their own reasons. But within the Inuit community, seal skins are a source of income. The seal meat is usually eaten at home, and in the past, they sold the skins—mostly to Europe. So for the Inuit people, the law has serious results. Are there any questions?

Student 2: I'm wondering what's ahead for the Inuit people— you know, what will their future be like? I mean, they can't control the laws in Europe, right?

Professor: That's true. However, the Inuit people are trying to change the law. They think that they should be able to sell seal products in Europe because they were some of the first people in North America. To them, the Inuit seal hunt is different from the rest of Canada's seal hunt. Other questions?

Student 3: Well, we're talking about ethics, and the Inuit people say it's fine for them to kill animals because people in other parts of the world kill animals, too. Personally, I don't agree. I'm a vegan, so I don't eat meat or any other animal products. I think all of us share the responsibility for taking care of animals—making sure nobody treats animals badly.

Professor: And that's a very important idea. If people really care about animals, should they use animals for food and clothing? Let's see . . . how many people in this class eat animal products like meat or eggs? Raise your hands. OK, it looks like most of you . . .

Track 19   Identifying Opinions   Page 167

Examples:
Extra Emphasis:
I do NOT want to WATCH this!
He gave an EXCELLENT presentation!

Special Language:
These beautiful animals have the amazing ability to see in the dark. Seal meat sounds disgusting, and the way people kill seals is awful!

Exploring Spoken English

Language Function: Making Comparisons

Track 20   A.   Page 169

Black Bear Research: Two Places and Two Methods

North American black bears are shy animals. They are fearful by nature, and will usually run away if they see or hear people. Because of this, it can be difficult for scientists to learn about these animals.

In order to study black bears, researchers in the state of New Jersey, USA, catch bears in traps. Then they sedate the bears with drugs, so they go to sleep and cannot move for a short time. Researchers then measure and weigh the bear, remove a tooth to find out the bear's age, and take blood to test for diseases. From these studies, researchers want to find out how many bears live in New Jersey, how long they live, and how many babies, or cubs, they produce.

Several hundred miles to the west, another black bear study is taking place in Minnesota, USA. There, Dr. Lynn Rogers and his team study bears that are completely awake. The bears know the researchers' voices and they are not afraid of the team. They still run away from other people, but with the help of a few grapes or nuts to keep the bears busy, Dr. Rogers can touch the animals to check their hearts, look at their teeth, and

change the radio or GPS equipment that the bears wear around their necks. He and his team can also walk or sit with the bears for hours and make videos to learn about the bears' everyday lives.

In both places, the main goal is the same—to make sure there is a healthy population of wild black bears. In contrast, the research methods and the kinds of information researchers are able to collect are quite different.

Lesson B
Building Vocabulary

Track 21   A. Using a Dictionary   Page 174

aggressive
attack
avoid
conflict
is worth
limited
reserve
save
scenery
wildlife

Track 22   B. Meaning from Context   Page 174

Marcy: Why did you decide to take this tour?
Hope: Well, I think gorillas and other kinds of wildlife are really interesting.
Marcy: I agree, and the scenery here is beautiful, too.
Hope: Yeah, all in all, this tour certainly is worth the cost.

Dan: I'm scared. The gorillas are so big! Do they ever attack humans?
Okello: Almost never. Gorillas are not aggressive. In fact, they usually try to avoid trouble. You don't often see a gorilla getting into a conflict with another animal.
Dan: Oh, really? Don't the male gorillas fight each other?
Okello: No. They usually just show their strength, and the other males go away. Anyway, the tour groups don't get too close to the gorillas, so we'll be fine.

Leandro: This part of the national park is a nature reserve, right?
Vanessa: That's right. It's illegal to hunt here, so the animals are pretty safe.
Leandro: Do you think that's going to save the mountain gorillas?
Vanessa: Maybe. There aren't many gorillas left, but the park helps to protect them.
Leandro: The park is a limited area, though. The gorillas can't go very far.
Vanessa: That's true, and I think it's the gorillas' biggest problem these days.

Developing Listening Skills
Listening: A Conversation

Track 23   A. Listening for Main Ideas   Page 176

Jack: It's been a long time, Dakarai! Tell us—how is life in Kariba Town?

Dakarai: Life is pretty good, Jack! The town is growing fast.

Jack: I suppose people go there because there's interesting wildlife and beautiful scenery.

Dakarai: Yes, and there are jobs there—mostly in tourism and fishing.

Jasmine: Sure—there must be a lot of fish in Lake Kariba.

Dakarai: That's right, Jasmine—a lot of fish, and it's a great place to go boating, so tourists love that. And of course tourists want to see the wildlife—elephants, leopards, baboons—a lot of different animals live there. Of course, that's also one of the problems in Kariba.

Jasmine: Why is it a problem?

Dakarai: It's the same problem as everywhere else, especially other places in Africa. There's a conflict between people and nature, right? People want to grow crops—animals want to eat the crops. People want to move onto the animals' land—the animals sometimes attack people.

Jack: Does that happen in Kariba? Are the animals aggressive?

Dakarai: Actually, animal attacks are not common. Most people in Kariba don't walk around at night, so they avoid any problems.

Jasmine: You don't go out at night?

Dakarai: Most of the time, no. In Kariba, daytime is for people, and at night, animals do anything they want. Elephants walk around outside your house, and leopards walk down the street.

Jasmine: Really? I can't imagine an elephant outside my house—not here in Athens!

Jack: She's right. There aren't a lot of wild animals in this part of Greece.

Dakarai: Well, Athens is a very old city, but there was no Kariba Town before the 1950s. The land around Kariba belonged to the animals.

Jasmine: And then they built the dam.

Dakarai: Yes, that's right. Then they built the dam. You know, when the water behind the dam began to rise, people had to save a lot of the animals. They went in boats to get them. Can you imagine? It's not easy to get wild baboons and zebras into a boat!

Jack: Wow! It's amazing that people did that!

Jasmine: So, how are the animals doing now?

Dakarai: Not very well, I'm afraid. There's a wildlife reserve near the lake, but it's a limited area, and a lot of people are hunting the animals.

Jasmine: That's awful! Why are they doing that?

Dakarai: Well, sometimes they're afraid. They think the animals might attack them. Most of the time, though, the people are hunting for food. A lot of people in Kariba Town are poor, and hunting is a way to feed their families.

Jack: I can see the problem, then.

Dakarai: It is a problem, but these wild animals are worth a lot to Zimbabwe. They're an important part of nature and of Africa, and they bring tourists into the country as well.

Jasmine: Tourists . . . and money from tourism.

Dakarai: That's right. Well, I should get going. I'm giving a talk in 20 minutes.

Jack: OK. It was great to see you again, Dakarai!

Jasmine: Yes, it really was, and good luck with your talk!

Dakarai: Thanks, it was good to see both of you, too.

Track 24 Pronunciation: Using Stress for Emphasis Page 177

Examples:
Showing Emotion:
A: Guess What?! I GOT the JOB!
B: Oh, that's GREAT!

To Give Meaning:
The land became a wildlife reserve AFTER it became a national park.

Track 25 A. Page 177

Jasmine: Really? I can't imagine an elephant outside my house—not here in Athens!

Jack: She's right. There aren't a lot of wild animals in this part of Greece.

Dakarai: Well, Athens is a very old city, but there was no Kariba Town before the 1950s. The land around Kariba belonged to the animals.

Jasmine: And then they built the dam.

Dakarai: Yes, that's right. Then they built the dam. You know, when the water behind the dam began to rise, people had to save a lot of the animals. They went in boats to get them. Can you imagine? It's not easy to get wild baboons and zebras into a boat!

Jack: Wow! It's amazing that people did that!

Exploring Spoken English

Grammar: Comparisons with *As . . . as*

Track 26 C. Page 179

Blind Bobcat Finds a Friend

A bobcat named Bear was lucky to be at a sanctuary that takes care of unwanted wildcats. He and the other animals at the sanctuary were not born in the wild, so they couldn't take care of themselves.

Bear had other problems, however. He was almost blind and very unfriendly toward other cats. Because of this, he was always alone. Then, workers at the sanctuary had an idea: Why not introduce him to Nairobi, a caracal who was just as unfriendly as Bear?

At first, a fence separated the two animals, but Bear knew "Robi" was there. He surprised everyone by acting friendly toward the caracal. Robi was not as friendly as Bear, but after a few weeks, the caracal seemed more comfortable with the other cat, so workers at the sanctuary opened the fence.

Now, Robi and Bear are best friends. Bear stays as close as possible to Robi and follows him around. If the bobcat loses Robi, he chirps until the caracal comes back. "Bear is so reliant on Robi," says Cheryl Tuller, director of the sanctuary, "Robi takes that as his job."

Unit 10: How We Communicate Lesson A

Building Vocabulary

Track 27 A. Using a Dictionary Page 184

access
basic
connect
contact
device
involved
message
represent
speed
unfortunately

1. Non-verbal communication is more basic than speaking a language. Babies, for example, are able to communicate with their parents by crying or smiling.
2. I'm not feeling well, so I need to contact my boss and tell her I can't work today.
3. An MP3 player is a popular device for playing music.
4. It's easy to access some kinds of information on the Internet.
5. Most computers are, unfortunately, quite expensive.
6. Many parts of the mouth are involved in speaking.
7. I tried to go online, but I couldn't connect to the Internet.
8. Anna didn't answer her phone, so I left a message for her.
9. For many people, the dollar sign represents money.
10. Information travels at a high speed from one computer to another computer.

Developing Listening Skills

Track 29   Pronunciation: Thought Groups   Page 186

Examples:
I'll call you later, / or I'll send you / an email.
My older brother / has always been / my best friend.

Track 30   A.   Page 186

With that software / on your computer, / you just need a device / that connects the computer / to a cell phone. Then the computer / uses the cell phone / to send messages / to a lot of different people. / It's pretty cool! / And the Internet / is not involved.

Track 31   B.   Page 186

1. Professor Jones / is the oldest professor / at the university.
2. I almost never / send a real letter / to anyone.
3. Lily has a phone, / but she doesn't have / a computer.
4. We had a good conversation / about our families.
5. Tom and Marsha / are my only friends / in the city.
6. The assignment / is to read a chapter / and write some questions / for discussion.

Listening: A News Report

Track 32   A. Listening for Main Ideas   Page 187

News Anchor: Our first story tonight comes from the world of information technology. It's about Ken Banks, a man who does a lot of work in Africa. And in many African countries, it's difficult to access the Internet.

Well, for many people, the Internet is a big part of the modern world. It represents information, speed, and convenience—things people everywhere want to have nowadays. In fact, the United Nations has said that being able to access the Internet is a basic human right. So according to the UN, it's the responsibility of countries to allow people to access the Internet—to get the information they need; to communicate with other people—all the different things we do online.

Well, unfortunately, a statement from the United Nations isn't enough in many places. In South Africa, for example, Ken Banks worked on a project at Kruger National Park. That's a huge wildlife reserve with elephants, giraffes—all kinds of animals. Of course, a lot of *people* live nearby, and the park wanted them to be involved in its work. They wanted to send people messages about meetings or about the animals in the park. They wanted to ask people for their opinions about park decisions. But all of this was a problem since people in that area could not access the Internet, so the park could not contact people that way.

On the other hand, a lot of people near the park did have cellular telephones, so Ken Banks invented software that he called Frontline SMS. With that software on your computer, you just need a device that connects the computer to a cell phone. Then the computer uses the cell phone to send messages to a lot of different people. It's pretty cool! And the Internet is not involved.

But that was just the beginning. People in many parts of the world had cellular phones, but no Internet service. They started to create their own ways to use Banks's software. Now, people use the software to send medical records to doctors, or to make payments on a loan without making a long trip to the bank. The software is used in many ways in over 70 countries, and the best part is . . . Ken Banks gives it away for free. He's happy to know that the software is helping in places that need it the most.

Exploring Spoken English

Language Function: Talking about Duration: The Present Perfect with *for* and *since*

Track 33   A.   Page 189

Layla: Hi, David. I don't think I've seen your car before.
David: It's an old one. I've had it since 2002.
Layla: It looks good. I've only had my car for two years, and it already looks old.
David: By the way, have you seen Alice recently?
Layla: No, I haven't seen her for several weeks.
David: Me neither. I sent her an email, but it bounced back.
Layla: Oh, she changed her email address. She's had a new one since February, I think.
David: Really? Could you give me her new email address?
Layla: Sure, no problem.

Speaking

Talking about the Recent Past

Track 34   C.   Page 191

Lionel: Have you written a letter to anyone recently?
Candice: Yes, I wrote a letter to my grandmother last week.
Lionel: A real letter—on paper?
Candice: Yes, my grandma doesn't use email.
Lionel: Oh, I see.
Candice: Have you used a video phone system recently?
Lionel: Yes, I talked with my brother last night. He's in Germany.

Lesson A and B Viewing: Touching the Stars

Before Viewing

Track 35   B. Using the Present Perfect Tense   Page 192

The Hubble Space Telescope has been in orbit since 1990, and people around the world have enjoyed the beautiful images that the telescope has sent back to Earth. One group of people, however, has had no opportunity to enjoy Hubble's discoveries—until recently. The National Aeronautics and Space Administration (NASA) has created a special book for people who are blind. It allows them to "see" images from Hubble and other telescopes with their fingers.

Lesson B

Building Vocabulary

Track 36   A. Meaning from Context   Page 194

Communications Satellites: How Many Is Too Many?

In one way or another, you probably use a satellite every day. If you watch TV, check the weather, or make a long-distance phone call, a satellite is involved. Satellites have changed the way we communicate, and they've also changed the space around Earth.

Back in the 1970s, former NASA scientist Donald Kessler realized that with thousands of satellites in orbit around the earth, a collision between two or more satellites was probable. He also knew that after such a collision, hundreds of small pieces of metal would be in orbit instead of two large satellites. Those pieces could cause even more collisions, and so on until the space around the earth was full of metal pieces. No satellite or spacecraft would be able to travel safely in space.

Then on February 10, 2009, a large communications satellite actually did collide with another satellite and added about 2000 pieces of space garbage to the cloud of objects in orbit. The response to the collision was an international conference to discuss ways to reduce the number of objects in orbit.

In 2007, the UN had already given some sensible advice to the world's space agencies. In order to prevent collisions, for example, countries should not use old satellites for missile target practice.

At the conference, scientists discussed ways to get rid of old satellites and metal pieces, such as a collector satellite to catch space garbage and bring it down into the earth's atmosphere to burn up. Such a solution, however, may be a long way away. Until then, space garbage will remain a danger to travel in space and communication on Earth.

Developing Listening Skills

Listening: A Telephone Conversation

Track 37   A. Note-Taking   Page 196

Jerry: Hello?
Todd: Hi, Jerry. It's Todd.
Jerry: Todd! It's great to hear from you. How was your trip?
Todd: The trip was fine, but when the plane landed in Cleveland, it was a little scary.
Jerry: Scary? What happened?
Todd: Well, after we landed, another plane crossed the runway right in front of our plane. I was worried about a collision, but I guess our pilot responded very quickly, so everything was fine.
Jerry: Wow! I'm glad to hear it! That must have been scary!
Todd: Yeah, it was. But, oh, I saw something interesting on the flight. It was right before the movie.

Jerry: Oh, yeah? What was it?
Todd: It was a commercial—like a TV advertisement—from the comedy network. It was about all the electronic garbage we've created—like old computers and printers and stuff—and how to get rid of it.
Jerry: I know how to get rid of it: Throw it away, right? And why is the comedy network making a TV commercial like that?
Todd: I guess if it's funny, more people will listen. The thing is— it's not OK to throw that kind of garbage away. Chemicals in the batteries can damage the environment, and there are metal parts for recycling. The metal can be worth a lot of money!
Jerry: Oh, yeah . . . I forgot about recycling. That sounds pretty sensible.
Todd: Right, and recycling reduces the amount of garbage we throw away.
Jerry: So, what did they talk about in the funny commercial?
Todd: Well, they made some jokes, of course, but they also talked about a Web site. You can go there and find out where and how to recycle your old electronic devices. I didn't realize we had a recycling center in our city.
Jerry: Really? Did you find that on the Web site?
Todd: Yep, and they talked about some companies that will take their products back when you're done with them. So if people can give their old computers and phones back to the company, it will prevent people from throwing them away and creating more garbage.
Jerry: Wow, that's an interesting idea.
Todd: Yeah, it is! So, did I miss anything interesting while I was gone?
Jerry: Actually, you did! Julie and Robert have decided to buy a new house, or maybe a condominium, so they . . .

After Listening

Track 38   A. Preparation   Page 197

Low-Tech Recycling of Electronics

Where? Ghana, Nigeria, India, China
How? People take apart electronic garbage by hand. They may also burn some of the garbage. Dangerous chemicals go into the air or onto the ground. Most of the electronic garbage comes from Europe, the United States, and other wealthy parts of the world.
Why? In the United States and other places, people either can't or don't want to send old electronic devices to landfills. Instead, they send them to recycling companies. Many recycling companies then send the garbage to other countries.

High-Tech Recycling of Electronics

Where? Ontario, Canada
How? A high-tech recycling company uses machines to separate different materials such as metal, glass, and plastic. Objects such as batteries with dangerous chemicals inside are removed by hand. Ontario has strong laws to protect the environment and charges a fee to recycle old electronics. That money makes the recycling company possible.
Why? A large amount of electronic garbage is produced nearby in the United States, and Canadian laws require recycling of electronics.

Unit 1: Butler School

Narrator:
Long ago, England was a land of country houses, palaces, gardens, and afternoon tea. Every real gentleman had servants, especially a butler. Just 70 years ago, there were tens of thousands of butlers in England, now there are only a few. So, where does one find a good butler nowadays?

The Ivor Spencer International School for Butler Administrators—of course!

Butler 1:
Good evening, sir. My name is Michael. I'm your butler.

Butler 2:
My name is Jose.

Butler 3:
I'm your butler.

Butler 4:
Can I bring you some refreshments, sir?

Butler 3:
I'm your butler.

Butler 5:
Good evening, sir.

Narrator:
It's the first day of class and the students are learning how to introduce themselves to their 'gentleman' or 'lady.'

A proper butler must also learn to carry himself correctly.

Ivor Spencer, School Owner:
Your champagne, my lady.

Butlers:
Your champagne, my lady.

Ivor Spencer:
No problem, sir.

Butlers:
No problem, sir.

Taxi Driver:
Butlers? I haven't seen a butler for a long time.

Narrator:
70 years ago, there were an estimated 30,000 butlers. Today there are fewer than 200. But, if Ivor Spencer has anything to say about it, that's going to change!

Butlers:
It's a pleasure, sir.

Ivor Spencer:
No problem, sir!

Butlers:
No problem, sir!

Ivor Spencer:
I'll fetch it immediately, sir.

Butlers:
I'll fetch it immediately, sir.

Narrator:
Ivor Spencer wants to use his school to bring back the butler to this land of tradition.

Ivor Spencer:
Good morning, everybody. Welcome to the Ivor Spencer School. We know you've come from all over the world and we appreciate you being here.

Narrator:
Future butlers must learn how to use the correct titles to refer to ambassadors, kings, queens, and lords. Over the next five weeks, 13 international students will have 86 lessons in the art of being a butler. If they succeed, they may work for a businessman, an important leader, or even a king. But, first, they have to graduate.

Mr. Spencer says that some people can't even last longer than the first few days.

Ivor Spencer:
On every course there are about two people that don't make it past the first two days.

Narrator:
This may come true for one student in the new group, David Marceau.

David Marceau, Butler Student:
Good morning, the Lee residence.

Practice makes perfect so hopefully, with a lot of practice, I'll be just as good as any other butler out there.

David Suter, Butler Student:
I just hope I'm going to be right for the job and hope I can do it.

Narrator:
It's important for students to keep their hopes up and practice, practice, practice!

Butlers:
It's a pleasure, sir.

Narrator:
The word 'butler' comes from the French word *'bouteiller'*, which means 'bottle carrier'. For new butlers, this can be difficult.

Ivor Spencer:
No problem, sir.

Butlers:
No problem, sir.

Butlers:
It's a pleasure, sir.

Ivor Spencer:
No problem, sir.

Butlers:
No problem, sir.

Ivor Spencer:
Your champagne, my lady.

Butlers:
Your champagne, my lady.

Narrator:
Things go better for everyone this time. It seems that all the practice is showing some results. Even David Marceau is showing improvement.

Butler 1:
Your champagne, my lord.

David Marceau:
It's on the floor, my lord.

Butler 1:
Good evening, sir.

Butler 2:
Good evening, sir.

David Suter:
Good evening, sir.

Narrator:
By the third week, students start to find out if they really can become butlers or not.

Butler 6:
I'm your butler.

David Suter:
Good evening, sir.

Ivor Spencer:
Go back.

David Marceau:
It's very difficult here. It's very difficult. The course isn't easy at all.

Good evening, sir. My name is David. And I am your butler. May I offer you some . . . May I offer you some . . .

Ivor Spencer:
Do that again, David.

David Marceau:
I have some problems and I have to deal with them.

Good evening, sir. My name is David and I am your butler.

Narrator:
David is not just having difficulty with the course; he also misses his friends and family back home.

David Marceau:
I miss my girlfriend very much. She's giving me support on the phone. I just talked to her last night, and things are okay and everything. Yes, I wish I was there right now.

Narrator:
There are a lot of secrets to being a good butler.

For example, did you know that you can iron a newspaper to make it look nice and avoid leaving ink everywhere?

Ivor Spencer does, and he teaches the class how to do it.

Ivor Spencer:
That's probably the only time the butler has . . . to read the newspaper. If you see a burnt newspaper, you know he's been, the butler's very interested.

Narrator:
Sometimes butlers need other unusual skills.
For example, they might need to deal with unwelcome guests. These butlers will be ready.

Butlers must also learn how to recognize quality products, or 'the finer things in life.' From the best tobacco pipes . . .

Pipe Expert:
It's not just a piece of wood. It's a piece of art.

Narrator:
. . . to expensive shoes . . . to, of course . . .

Shopkeeper:
Welcome to the house of *Moet et Chandon*.

Narrator:
. . . champagne.

Shopkeeper:
Sante! To champagne.

Narrator:
Graduation day arrives.

Ivor Spencer:
David, you've come a long way. We appreciate it.

Narrator:
Everyone gets their certificates—even David.

After, the students have a small party.

Ivor Spencer:
Good health everybody.

David Suter:
I did it!

Narrator:
Before they came here, these young men and women drove buses, worked with computers, or worked in restaurants or stores.

Now they are part of a very old English tradition.

The Ivor Spencer School for Butler Administrators has done its job well!

Unit 2: Nubian Wedding

Narrator:
It is modern, yet firmly rooted in the past. The Nubian wedding ritual, shared by the entire village . . . for seven days and nights.

The air is perfumed by incense and filled with the sound of beating drums, and joyful Nubian songs.

Two years ago Sherrif's family told him it was time to get married. He visited every home in the village looking for the right girl. Then, with one look at Abeer, he ran home to tell his mother he had found his bride. They didn't meet again until just before their Muslim wedding.

After the legal papers are signed, seven days of celebration begin. Each day, early in the morning the party spills into the village streets. The bride becomes a canvas — painted from head to toe with henna. One day before the ceremony, the groom's bed is taken outside to be bathed in sandalwood incense. Sherrif is also perfumed. The scents, which will last for weeks, are meant to get his blood moving and give him stamina.

The Nubians traditionally lived along the banks of the Nile River in what is now southern Egypt and the Sudan. But in the 1960s, that changed. In Egypt, the Nubian population was moved by the Egyptian government and their ancient lands were flooded when the Aswan Dam was built.

Mohammed Nour migrated here at the age of 12. His family left their mud-brick home for one of cement built by the government.

Mohammed Nour:
Even though there, in the old village, there was no electricity or means of transportation like we have here now, still life there was better. There we used to keep our Nubian traditions and Nubian language. Nubian language could be endangered here today.

Narrator:
On the final night of the wedding, the village is served a feast of meat and rice in front of the groom's house.

Armed with a sword and whip, the groom leaves his parents' home and leads his neighbors through the streets chanting Islamic songs.

Well after midnight, the groom at last picks up the bride and they arrive at the party. They spend all night dancing and singing from sunset to noon.

The word 'Nubia' derives from an ancient term for 'gold' and refers to the gold mines for which the area was once famous. That gold still shines today . . . as the bride is draped with jewelry . . . as if she were royalty.

It's now past three in the morning . . . but by Nubian standards the party has just begun.

After the exchange of rings, mother kisses her son and his new bride as they begin their life together, carrying on their ancient customs.

Egyptian by nationality, but Nubian by tradition.

Unit 3: Treasures in Old San Juan

Narrator:
San Juan is the second oldest European-founded city in the Americas. People first came to live here in 1521. Surrounded by a huge wall and filled with narrow streets, it's a typical colonial city. But make no mistake, Old San Juan is not a museum. It's a wonderful, colorful place . . . very much alive.

Ricardo Rivera is just one of thousands of people who call Old San Juan home.

Ricardo Rivera, Old San Juan Resident
It's probably the cultural center of Puerto Rico in a lot of ways. There's music . . . There's a lot of young artists. A lot of bohemian writers, a lot of cultural activity happens in Old San Juan.

Narrator:
It's an attractive neighborhood, he says, because many of the beautiful historic buildings have been returned to their original condition.

Ricardo Alegría is an archaeologist who helped to bring the historic past of Old San Juan alive again.

Ricardo Alegría, Archaeologist and Old San Juan Resident:
I am proud of what we've done, because in the 50s, San Juan was becoming a slum area . . . A lot of bars and the houses . . . some of the buildings were in really bad shape.

Narrator:
Today those buildings are mostly in wonderful condition. And so are Old San Juan's many fortresses.

The most impressive is Fuerte San Felipe del Morro. It was built by the Spanish, starting around 1540, to defend the city from attack by sea.

The church of San Jose, on which work started in 1532, is the second oldest known church in the Western Hemisphere.

Around the corner, the Plaza San Jose . . . where you find a statue of explorer Ponce de Leon . . . made from bronze from a British cannon.

Down the street, La Fortaleza . . . another fortress, is now used as the governor's house.

Everywhere you turn, there are reminders of San Juan's adventure-filled past.

Over the centuries, San Juan was often attacked by its enemies. These days, tourists fill the streets in search of old-world charm and the pleasant climate.

Domingo Deleon, Tour Guide:
The whole year round we have nice weather here. Nice weather, the temperatures are 75-77-80, ya know?

Narrator:
So, San Juan is a major vacation destination. In fact, this is one of the busiest ports for cruise ships in the entire Caribbean. More than a million visitors a year arrive on these luxury liners.

Tourist:
It's beautiful, beautiful beaches, a lot of greenery, very friendly people!

Narrator:
Friendly . . . for visitors getting to know Puerto Rican culture . . . and for the people who live here year round.

Ricardo Rivera:
Old San Juan is like a small neighborhood, in a lot of ways. You live here and you never use your car. You walk to the supermarket, you know the-the guy that sells you your vegetables. And everybody says 'hello.' It's [a] very small town.

Unit 4: Tornado Chase

Narrator:
June 24, 2003: Storm chaser Tim Samaras is in tornado alley looking for trouble.

Tim Samaras, Stormchaser:
This thing turned into a big gust front.

Narrator:
His goal: to place as many scientific probes as possible directly in the path of a giant twister.

The trick: do it without getting killed.

The perfect conditions are forming near a tiny town called Manchester. Tim and his teammates drive towards an enormous thunder cloud. About seven miles out, a tornado starts taking shape.

He tries to get closer, but no roads lead in the right direction.

Tim Samaras:
Let's take this and go up and around.

Radio Announcer:
This is a dangerous storm . . . take shelter immediately.

Tim Samaras:
I'm going to wait until we get the right angle.

Narrator:
He outraces the tornado for a few miles.

Tim Samaras:
We took the road heading east, basically going right into the path of the tornado.

Narrator:
One probe down, five to go.

Tim Samaras:
We're gonna get hit, we're gonna get hit!

Narrator:
The chasers estimate it's at least a F-4 tornado, with winds over 200 miles an hour.

A twister this fierce can destroy a well-built house and turn a mobile home into a missile.

Tim's probes will record wind speed, barometric pressure, and other data . . . if the tornado sweeps directly overhead. The more he deploys, the better the chances.

But remaining close to a twister is a dangerous game. The tornado destroys a nearby farmhouse—a reminder of what 200-mile-an-hour winds can do. Still, Tim is determined to deploy the last of his six probes.

Tim Samaras:
Let's drop one more!

Man:
Tim, we don't have time. . . we don't have time . . . we don't have time . . . seriously.

Tim Samaras:
He was saying that, but I was thinking something else. I was already out of the car, I'd gotten the probe, had put it on the ground, and I jumped in, and I deployed in five to seven seconds.

Narrator:
Then suddenly, the tornado turns on them.

Man:
It's coming back on the road . . . it's coming right at us, too!

Narrator:
Twisters can accelerate at speeds of 70 miles an hour. This one is only 100 yards away and approaching fast.

Man:
Listen to it!

Narrator:
If it catches up, it will throw their van through the air, then crush it like a tin can. The driver goes as fast as he can, but the tornado seems to be getting closer. The twister chases the van down the road.

Then, at the very last second, turns away and loses power. They escape unharmed.

Unit 5: Forbidden Fruit

Narrator:
Here in Malaysian Borneo, a seasonal invasion is underway. Staff at hotels watch nervously for a food that is smelly, awful, and loved by millions. Meet the durian fruit. Its smell is hard to describe.

Audrey, Hotel Worker:
It smells like a rotten fish and custard.

Person 1:
A rubbish dump.

Edward, Hotel Worker:
Bleu cheese.

Person 2:
Perhaps a dead dog.

Narrator:
Other cultures love foods that smell strongly. Cheese, a favorite in the West, is actually rotted milk . . . a smell people in Asia find disgusting. Like cheese in France, durian is precious in Southeast Asia. Some believe it's worth killing for.

Durian trees don't bear fruit until they're 15 years old. A single durian can cost as much as 50 dollars American.

Here in Kuching, the capital of Malaysian Borneo, hotels are on the front lines of the durian war. When the fruit is in season, hotel managers maintain a constant vigil to keep it out. For them, the problem is really about money. One smelly durian fruit can scare off a hotel full of customers.

Edward:
So it goes into the curtains. It sticks into the carpet. It sticks into the bedspreads.

Narrator:
That doesn't stop people from trying to smuggle it in.

Audrey:
We can immediately smell it, and they always deny it, but we know that they've got them.

Narrator:
Every hotel has its own method of dealing with a durian alert.

Edward:
There are only two methods of getting rid of the smell we found. One is charcoal. Charcoal absorbs the smell. And the other . . . that takes quite a long time. And the other one . . . we've got an ionizer that . . . it's an

industrialized one, and within three hours we can pull the smell out of the room.

Audrey:
Please no durians here, not in the hotel. Outside . . . in the fresh air you can do it. But definitely not in here.

Narrator:
In Borneo, visitors can decide for themselves if the durian is delicious, or just plain disgusting . . . as long as they do their taste testing outdoors.

Unit 6: Don't Believe Your Eyes!

Narrator:
Camogli looks just like any other town on the Italian coast. The little colored houses face the sea and the sun shines on them. But, if you look carefully, you'll see something very interesting.

In the town of Camogli, there are many things that seem real . . . but they're not.

This fishing village near Genoa is full of *trompe l'oeil*—a type of art in which nothing is what it seems to be.

For example, in this particular village, windows open—in solid walls. There seems to be elaborate stonework—but it isn't stonework—it's paint! And while some flowers die, other flowers live for years. Why? Because they're painted on the building!

In the past, Camogli's fishermen used to paint their houses in bright colors and unusual designs. They did this so that they could easily see their homes from the water.

Then, in the 1700s, this style of art became a way to make small, simple buildings look grand and seem like they cost a lot of money.

Now, there are still thousands of *trompe l'oeil* houses in this area. But only a few artists still paint them.

Raffaella Stracca is one of these artists. She learned this style of painting from her grandmother. Raffaella uses a mixture of old and new methods to create her work.

Raffaella Stracca, Artist:
You find a lot of these painted facades in the area of Liguria a lot. But for a while, it seemed like no one was doing them anymore.

Narrator:
It takes a long time to become a good *trompe l'oeil* painter. Rafaella has worked for 20 years to be able to paint stone so well that it looks real—even if you're close to it.

Like most painters, Raffaella learned *trompe l'oeil* from other artists, not in a school. But these days, there are fewer artists, fewer teachers, and fewer places to learn the technique.

In Florence, The Palazzo Spinelli Art School has one of the few *trompe l'oeil* programs available. Painters work a full year to learn how to make everything from *trompe l'oeil* stonework to fake doors.

Even though most students aren't from Italy, they understand that the technique is a very Italian tradition.

Helga Hansen, Art Student:
I haven't seen anywhere else in the world as much of *trompe l'oeil* and mural painting as much as here in Italy.

Narrator:
Carlo Pere is one artist who studied *trompe l'oeil* and made a business out of it. His customers are often people who live in small houses or city apartments. They want to buy Pere's *trompe l'oeil* terraces and balconies to improve the appearance of their homes.

Carlo feels that *trompe l'oeil* brings something unexpected to a new place.

Carlo Pere, Artist:
Trompe l'oeil means bringing the central city of Milan to the sea, or the sea to the mountains . . . or even the mountains to the sea.

Narrator:
Carlo's style comes from history. He uses an art book from the 1300s to study the technique. He uses only traditional-style paints and mixes them by hand.

He does all of this for one reason: to protect the *trompe l'oeil* traditions.

Carlo Pere:
It's easy to see. If we lose the *trompe l'oeil* tradition, then very little of Camogli's culture will remain. We'll have museums, but that's not much. Culture should be seen.

Narrator:
Fortunately, in this part of Italy, you can still see the local culture everywhere. It's in the street, in the bay, and in the cafés of the town. But remember, in Camogli what you see, might not be what you think it is . . . so don't always believe your eyes!

Unit 7: Exploration of the Solar System

Narrator:
Since the beginning of space exploration in the 1950s, dozens of celestial bodies in the solar system have received a visit from probes.

The Sun itself was examined in 1990 by the probe *Ulysses*, which studied the solar wind, among other things.

Mercury, the planet closest to the Sun, was photographed by *Mariner 10*, but the probe was able to map only 45 percent of the planet's surface.

We know more about Venus, since it has been observed by many probes. The most recent, *Magellan*, mapped 98 percent of the surface of Venus, revealing a rather flat relief.

Mars, which presents conditions favorable to human settlement, has been the focus of particular attention. A dozen probes have already studied it.

Jupiter, the largest planet in the solar system, is also well known. The *Pioneer 10* and *Pioneer 11* probes, launched in the 1970s, revealed that Jupiter is a gas giant with no solid surface. A few years later, the *Voyager 1* and *Voyager 2* probes photographed the violent storms that stir up its thick atmosphere.

Between 1995 and 2003, the *Galileo* probe took a close look at the moons of Jupiter, particularly Europa.

The *Pioneer 11* probe and the *Voyager* probes also observed Saturn. Data from these probes showed that the planet's rings are made up of thousands of small rings.

The *Voyager 2* probe continued toward Uranus, then Neptune, which it flew by in 1989.

Pluto still has not been studied by a probe. The probe *New Horizons* was launched in 2006; it will start sending data back to Earth in 2015.

Unit 8: Urban Art

Narrator:
A train tunnel in America's capital city is a gritty gallery. The signatures, or "tags," of graffiti artists are taken to a new level with broader strokes and bolder colors.

It is Washington D.C.'s wall of fame, and Nick Posada's work is here. "Tale" is his tag.

Nick Posada, Graffiti Artist:
This is what happens when nobody respects any-any type of work that someone spent their-their paint and their time on. This is what the Wall of Fame in D.C. has come to.

Narrator:
Even on such a public canvas, there are rules to be followed in the world of graffiti, and Posada has learned them well in the six years that he's been "tagging up."

Nick Posada:
You got-you got people that understand color and understand what's aesthetically pleasing and want their stuff to stand out, so you would use colors that contrast one another. Ah, my piece is still there. I did this like '99.

Narrator:
But Nick's work is also here at the Govinda Gallery in Georgetown, thanks to owner Chris Murray.

Chris Murray, Govinda Gallery:
Graffiti art has certainly brought to public art a whole new dimension because public art, as we know it, was always commissioned. Graffiti art was spontaneous, had nothing to do with any transaction. It feels fast, it feels bright, it feels very inventive.

Narrator:
Murray believes that graffiti is just one more step in the evolution of pop art.

And the works have sold. Mostly to young people, but also to longtime collectors of pop art. They could appreciate graffiti in a safe, traditional setting—and they liked it.

Good for the artists, too.

Chris Murray:
It was a real reversal for them because they're used to being vilified, and now they're being enjoyed, and that's a good thing.

Narrator:
Beauty may always remain in the beholder's eye. But art is about exploration and discovery. Even if it's just in a nearby city street.

Unit 9: Horses

Narrator:
Speed . . . strength . . . and power. Thousands of years before humans invented cars and airplanes, it was the horse who allowed us to go faster, go farther, and explore the world.

Horses belong to the family of mammals called *Equidae*, along with zebras and donkeys.

Like their close relatives, horses adapted to live in open country, eating grass, and using sheer speed to escape predators. They're highly social and live in herds, which also helps protect against enemies.

At first, humans were just one of the many hunters that preyed on the horse.

But some 4000 years ago, in central Asia, everything changed. Whether it was inspiration . . . or an experiment . . . or a teen-aged game, someone jumped onto a horse's back. From then on, human history was set to the pounding sound of horse's hooves. Whether they were *conquistadors* or cowboys—they owe their adventures to the same animal.

Horses first lived in the forests of North America. About a million years ago, some crossed land bridges, spreading to Asia and Europe. These pioneers saved their species. About 8000 years ago, either climate change or over-hunting by early humans did its damage—and the last horses in America died out. Horses sailed back to their native land in the 1500s, carried in the ships of Spanish explorers.

Soon Native Americans were trading with the Spanish, eager to own these amazing new animals. The descendants of their horses live on, in wild herds of mustangs, which live in the American West today.

As horses became valuable workers, people began to breed them for different jobs. Over a hundred different breeds of domestic horses are now recognized, but they all belong to the same species, *Equus caballus*.

Horses are classified based on their height, which is measured in hands—a unit of four inches, or literally the width of a human hand. Ponies are simply small horses—standing less than 14.2 hands, or just under five feet, at the shoulder. Draft horses are heavily built, with enough strength to pull weighty loads, and can stand over 19 hands, or six and a half feet high. Light horses such as racehorses fall in between.

Over the last century, machines have taken over most of the work that horses used to do. Yet there are more horses alive today than during the 1800s—some 62 million. Horses still offer us an important connection to the natural world—partners to work and play with—and the touch of something wild.

Unit 10: Touching the Stars

Narrator:
From the endless reaches of space, images that delight the eye are admired in a most unlikely place. The Colorado School for the Deaf and Blind . . .

Student 1:
Are these stars?

Narrator:
Where students have the universe at their fingertips.

Student 2:
I got Jupiter.

Student 3:
The outlines of these show the arms of the galaxies.

Student 4:
Let's see, I see those moons, and um, I see like, those stars.

Narrator:
Images taken by the Hubble space telescope have found their way into a classroom for students with different levels of vision loss.

These are the critics who were chosen to review a new book that displays some of the most spectacular space images ever produced.

Student 3:
Now it says red for sulfur, green for hydrogen, and blue for oxygen. But the problem with that is I can't tell the different color of the gases, these lines are all the same.

Narrator:
The book is called *Touch The Universe, a NASA Braille Book of Astronomy*.

Each photo comes with a transparent plastic sheet overlay covered with raised dots and ridges, giving visually impaired readers a feel for the limitless reaches of space.

Nimer Jaber, Student
I've always wondered about space you know, what it feels like what it-you know what, how big it really was.

Noreen Grice, Author:
You can't just reach out and touch the stars, nobody can, but we can bring it to people's fingertips, we can bring images that people might have only imagined; and we can bring it close to them so people can understand what these objects are in the universe, and I think better understand their place within the universe.

Narrator:
When asked to field test prototypes of the book, the students were happy just to be involved.

Then they realized their opinions would shape the way the book was presented to people who are blind around the world.

Ben Wentworth, Teacher:
Then they started tearing the images up.

Narrator:
Part of the problem with early versions of the plastic overlays is that they had touch points for everything in the photograph.

Fingers got lost in a galaxy of dots and ridges. Later versions of the book provided more room to maneuver.

Nimer Jaber:
It has great pictures, I can-you know-you can feel them better, you could-you know-you know what their shapes are.

Narrator:
Revisions were duly noted . . .

Noreen Grice:
All right, I-I can-I can make the change in the plate.

Student 3:
And that's really all I'm really suggesting to have.

Narrator:
Exactly what these students "see" in their mind's eye remains a mystery for sighted people.

Student 1:
This one reminds me of onion rings.

Narrator:
Still, it's clear that with each raised ridge and dot, an image of space that makes sense reveals itself.

Student 5:
That's pretty cool.

Ben Wentworth:
To get the kids to say, oh that's what you're seeing.
I think that's what's so unique about the Hubble Book.

Narrator:
The images provided by the Hubble space telescope continue to astonish and amaze, and provide a window on the wonders of space, no matter how you see them.